Advance Praise for *Up Your Game*

"*Up Your Game* combines notable insight with David Bradford's real-world experience. David skillfully combines his knowledge of social media with six timeless precepts that will help anyone build a strong foundation for success in life and business."

—Eric Schmidt, Executive Chairman, Google

"I have known David Bradford for over 25 years and consider him one of my dearest friends. He is indeed a master at building and maintaining important relationships. This book tells the world his secrets to this and many of his other successes. I highly recommend you read this great work."

—Steve Young, NFL Hall of Fame, Founder
and Managing Director, HGGC

"I cannot wait to give a copy of this book to each of my kids. Why? One, because I want them to know and learn how to direct their energies in building their careers, and two, I want them to see how much energy is really involved in achieving success! As David points out, it is well-directed effort that makes the difference. *Up Your Game* is the perfect roadmap for anyone who wants to understand the roots of real and lasting success."

—Dave Checketts, CEO and Chairman of
Legends Hospitality Management

"David Bradford exudes energy, passion, and his amazing life and professional principles in *Up Your Game*. Personally, I wouldn't be where I am without him, and my company, HireVue, wouldn't be where it is without him. Heck, the technology world wouldn't be where it is without him. If Bradford's UP Principles are the key to his success, this book needs to be on everyone's shelf—complete with highlights and notes in the margins."

—Mark Newman, Founder and CEO, HireVue

"David is a self-made-connected-man. He knows how to do it, and he's shared his methods so simply and eloquently within. A must-read for any serious entrepreneur in this day and age."

— Shawn Nelson, Founder of @Lovesac, First winner of Richard Branson's Rebel Billionaire contest

"After surviving over 50 years in show business, I've found that these principles that David presents in this book are not only important in a long-lasting pursuit of business, but essential in all aspects of life."

—Donny Osmond, Actor, Singer

"I have known and worked with David Bradford in the technology sector of our economy for over 20 years. David's *Up Your Game* is a well-written guide on becoming and remaining competitive in today's increasingly interconnected business environment. *Up Your Game* provides straightforward and easy-to-execute strategies to improve your networking skills, regardless of your age or circumstance."

—Orrin G. Hatch, United States Senator

"From State Golf Champion to CEO of two companies named among America's Most Promising, to Hall of Fame Inductee, David has seemingly done it all, while helping those around him succeed, as well. This book tells you how a small-town Montana kid did it and, more importantly, how you can do it too. Anyone in business, whatever the current trajectory of their careers, can really take it to the next level by reading *Up Your Game* and incorporating the principles outlined."

—Sharlene W. Hawkes, President, RMS Military Productions,
Former ESPN Sportscaster, Miss America 1985

"When it comes to connecting with the right people to build great teams and great organizations, David Bradford stands on top of the podium. Regardless of what stage of your career you find yourself in, the proven principles in *Up Your Game* are too valuable to pass up."

—Peter Vidmar, Olympic Gold Medalist,
Chairman, USA Gymnastics

"Successful entrepreneurs know that starting and scaling a business is most effective when you have a solid network to rely upon. *Up Your Game* is the must-read guide for authentic, natural, network-building success."

—Richie Norton, bestselling author of *The Power
of Starting Something Stupid*

"David Bradford's book is an insightful distillation of the learnings of decades of attentive observation from his vantage within the war rooms of some of America's iconic entrepreneurial enterprises."

—Steve Lund, Chairman, Nu Skin Enterprises

"*Up Your Game* is truly insightful and is as important to C-Level Executives as it is to college students. In this book, David masterfully teaches the art of connecting and building deep and lasting business relationships that become actionable in real-world settings. He is a man that not only has talked the talk but has walked the walk."

—Ray Bingham, Director, General Atlantic
and Former CEO, Cadence Design

"David Bradford's book outlines a pragmatic approach and guide to developing business relationships and using social networks and media to advance entrepreneurial success."

—Larry Sonsini, Chairman, Wilson, Sonsini

"*Up Your Game* is a truly unique take on principles that we all intuitively know are important but search for ways to implement them. In this book, David has clearly delineated a series of amazing steps that anyone can take to improve their lot in business or in life in general. If one studies and incorporates his 6 Up Principles, it can be a game changer for one's career."

—Scott McNealy, Founder and CEO, Sun Microsystems,
Chairman, Wayin

"After reading David's book, I am feeling completely Up and ready to implement the Six Up Principles. And after knowing the amazing David Bradford personally for many decades, I know that *everyone* can benefit from his superb ideas that make this the ultimate book for those who want to accelerate their move up to the top of any organization."

—Lew Cramer, former CEO, World Trade Center of Utah

"*Up Your Game* lays out a current and practical roadmap to building personal and professional relationships with integrity and purpose. A must read for all ages living or operating in this interconnected world."

—Scott R. Cutler, EVP & Head of Global Listings, IntercontinentalExchange | NYSE

"David has always had a passion for hiring top talent and connecting people to opportunity. It is reflected in the people and teams he has built at outstanding companies like Novell, Fusion-io and, more recently, HireVue. *Up Your Game* tells the story of how he gets it done."

—Steve Wozniak, Inventor of the Apple computer, Chief Scientist, Fusion-io

"Success in business—and in life—revolves around relationships with others; Bradford describes how one can effectively and meaningfully connect with others. The combination of his experience and insights makes *Up Your Game* a valuable guide."

—Mitt Romney, 2012 Republican Presidential Nominee, Former Govenor of Massachusetts

"David Bradford is a truly remarkable person who has written an equally amazing book. *Up Your Game* is simultaneously filled with deep insight as well as practical application. No one understands networking better than David, and no one is more connected. In this engaging book, he shares how he does it—and how we might do it too."

—Stephen M. R. Covey, author of *New York Times* and # 1 *Wall Street Journal* bestseller, *The Speed of Trust*, and co-author of *Smart Trust*

"David Bradford's ability to network comes naturally and serves as a resource that produced great success both at Novell and, in the years since, far beyond. I am delighted to see him share his finely honed secrets with the rest of the world."

—Carine Strom Clark, CEO of Allegiance, Inc., Former CMO of Symantec

YOUR GAME

Sourced Media Books
29 Via Regalo
San Clemente, CA 92673
www.sourcedmediabooks.com

Life Science Publishers
1216 South 1580 West, Ste. A
Orem, UT 84058
www.lifesciencepublishers.com

ISBN-13: 978-1-937458-74-4

Printed in the United States of America.

This publication is designed to provide entertainment value and is sold with the understanding that the publisher is not engaged in rendering legal, accounting, or other professional advice of any kind. If legal advice or other expert assistance is required, the services of a competent professional person should be sought.

—From a Declaration of Principles jointly adopted by a
Committee of the American Bar Association and a
Committee of Publishers and Associations

YOUR GAME

6 TIMELESS PRINCIPLES FOR NETWORKING YOUR WAY TO THE TOP

DAVID BRADFORD

CONTENTS

FOREWORD

LARRY KING AND SHAWN KING

Every now and then, someone walks into your life and you say to yourself: "Boy, I am glad I know that guy." Our family has been privileged to know David Bradford for nearly 30 years.

When my wife, Shawn, and I were asked to write the foreword to his exciting new book, we were most happy to do so. David has gone from being a young child living in poverty to being one of the most sincere, successful, and connected guys in the world. He is truly the Human Internet.

Over the years, we have interacted closely with David on a variety of business matters. When we launched Ora.TV, David gave us some great counsel and, of course, connections. More recently, as we have become involved in theBusinessCampus. com, we have reached out again to David for guidance. He has been kind enough to serve on the advisory board for this endeavor, where he has added tremendous value. I have been delighted to reciprocate by serving as a member of David's advisory board at HireVue and even introduced the video where he was featured as the newest member of the Utah Technology Hall of Fame. As David writes about so eloquently in his book, there is a law of reciprocity in the Universe, and this has been very beneficial to both sides of our business relationship.

Perhaps more importantly, we have come to know David on a very personal level and know that he is someone who lives the six "Up Principles" that he espouses in his book. One quick example—In January of 2013, Shawn's uncle, Bobby Engemann, passed away. Bobby was known far and wide as one of the members of the famous Lettermen singing group. My father-in-law, Karl Engemann, Shawn's dad, was then Vice President of Artist & Repertoire (A&R) at Capitol Records. He was instrumental in the success of the Lettermen. In June of 2013, Karl, Shawn, and I hosted a wonderful concert commemorating Bobby's life. David "Showed Up" as he often does, despite a ton of other responsibilities, with his family and camera in tow. Not only did we feel his support, but he also took a number of great photos. But then, in his extraordinary way, David "Followed Up." He created a gorgeous photobook of the evening and gave a number of copies to our family members. This is a memory that we will treasure forever.

David is the type of person that always takes the extra step. People think about doing nice things for others. Fleeting moments run through all of our minds about reaching out and helping others, but somehow David actually does them. As David points out so strongly in his book, the more you give, the more you get. David lives his first principle of "Starting Up" your network by giving first to others. This is what makes *Up Your Game* an important work. It is written by someone who doesn't just talk the talk—it was created by someone who walks the walk.

This is an amazing read. The six Up Principles are tried-and-true calls to action—things we can actively do to change our perspectives about networking and building relationships.

As explained more fully in the book, some of David's key assets are the tools of online communication that we have come to know as "social media." Many books that feature social media are written by self-anointed social media gurus. This book is different. It is written by a CEO who has lived and implemented the six Up Principles. David understands and implements social media perhaps better than any CEO out there.

Up Your Game will be an outstanding guidepost for new graduates who are seeking their first great job opportunity. Additionally, it will help any CEO trying to successfully navigate the world of social media in order to build key business partnerships and hire the best talent in the world. It will also be of great value to people trying to advance their careers, regardless of where they are in their journey.

If you have ever wondered how to connect with others in a meaningful way and make those relationships actionable, this is the book for you. *Up Your Game* outlines a marvelous game plan on how to succeed in life and business.

INTRODUCTION

FROM BOTTLE CAP KID TO CEO

In the summer of 2013, I was getting ready to address a group of 350 young adults at Ardingly College in England. My subject: "How to build your own billion-dollar network."

My older sister, who was the conference organizer, arose to introduce me. She had invited me there to be the conference keynote speaker to help inspire these young people to achieve success in their business careers. So, I thought she was going to brag about her little brother and read from the backgrounder I had assembled about myself. It included some fun facts about my business career—hiring the inventor of the Apple computer, Steve Wozniak, at Fusion-io; receiving a glowing endorsement from Google Chairman, Eric Schmidt, when I was announced as CEO of HireVue; raising over $150 million dollars from the world's top VC's; and being inducted into the Utah Technology Hall of Fame. But I did not hear any of that.

There was a palpable buzz as Patcee rose to the front of the room. "Let me tell you about my little brother David," she began. And then, much to my surprise, tears sprang to her eyes. She paused for a long moment and then spoke. "You see, my brother, David, was the Bottle Cap Kid."

The Bottle Cap Kid

As children living in Burbank, California, we had very few material things. My brothers and sisters and I had an alcoholic father who, after some early success in his career, bounced from job to job. There were long, depressing periods when, in order to get our next meal, we were reliant on our church welfare program.

Toys were scarce, so we were forced to develop our own games. One of them was "Bottle Cap Armies." The year was 1955. World War II had ended just a decade earlier, so the strategy of building and deploying armies was at the forefront of our minds. Together with my brother and his friend, we created a game similar to Risk—but with bottle caps.

First, we bent the caps into shapes so they would stand up. We then protected our armies of bottle caps by placing them behind wooden blocks. The next step of our grand game was to steal Mom's vacuum cleaner hoses and add in some marbles we found lying around. We rolled the marbles through the vacuum hoses and crashed them into the wooden barricades we had erected to protect our armies. We loved it.

As the game developed, we found ourselves in need of additional armies. We couldn't afford to buy the bottles to take the caps, but we knew one place that had plenty.

Joe's Market, on Magnolia Boulevard in Burbank, was about two blocks away from our place. Joe, the owner, had dark hair, a stout build, and a stern character—but, on occasion, he broke out into a welcoming grin. My older brother and sisters and I would go to Joe's to buy chewing gum when we could scratch up a couple of pennies. I didn't care much for the chewing gum, but what excited me about going to Joe's market was the soda pop dispenser. It contained something I treasured—bottle caps.

A red soda machine stood four feet off the ground near the entrance to Joe's Market. Rows and rows of glass pop bottles sat in the bottom of that dispenser in beds of ice. When Joe's customers wanted a bottle of soda, they would reach inside the large canister and pull out a cold one, then pop off the bottle cap into the bottle cap catcher that was mounted on the side of the machine.

Joe emptied the bottle cap catcher into the trash once or twice a day. But in my five-year-old mind, there was a much better use for those caps. You see, they came in a bunch of different varieties—Dad's Root Beer, Canada Dry Ginger Ale, Cream Soda, Grape Nehi, Orange Nesbitts, and my personal favorite bottle cap: Royal Crown Cola. Our post-World War II minds envisioned building armies of bottle caps—armies of each different variety. So, if Joe was just going to throw those bent and sticky bottle caps away, we were going to find a way to get the mother lode.

One day, I summoned up what seemed to me to be superhuman courage. Joe was a big man and wildly intimidating to my young eyes, but I wanted those bottle caps enough to fight my fear. With all of the courage I could muster, I asked Joe if we could please have the caps from the bottle cap catcher. He gave me a strange look but agreed. So every time I came into the store, Joe walked over to the soda machine and emptied handfuls of bottle caps into an old brown bag that I brought with me to the store. I then walked home with my ragged sack, emptied my precious treasure onto my bedroom floor, and began the process of sorting the caps into their respective armies. Bottle Cap Armies was a "go," and that's how I earned the nickname, "The Bottle Cap Kid."

The Up Principles

I learned some valuable lessons from those bottle caps and my visits to Joe's Market. In Burbank. My life lessons continued when, much to our surprise, Dad came home from work one day when I was ten years old and announced to the family that we were moving to Montana. At that point in my young life, I was suddenly thrust from the relatively comfortable confines of Southern California to a small town in Montana, where I was forced to adapt to a dramatically new social environment. Those lessons served me well throughout my life. They have taught me how to network with people to achieve the goals I envision for myself and the companies I manage. They have kept me buoyed up and moving forward during difficult times in my life. They have made me a better business manager, a better father, a better friend, and a better man. They have allowed me to go from being a disconnected guy in Red Lodge, Montana, to the leader of not one but two companies that the *Wall Street Journal* and *Forbes* named as among the Top Ten "Most Promising Companies in America." They are principles that I see practiced by the best CEOs with whom I have had the pleasure of interacting—folks like Eric Schmidt, Ray Noorda, Steve Jobs, and Bill Gates. They are six tried-and-true calls to action—things we can actively do to change our perspectives about networking and building relationships. I call them my "Up Principles."

- First, *Start Up.* Recognize that networking is more about giving than receiving. When people know you care about them and are really genuinely interested in helping them, the law of reciprocity kicks in. The more you give to any relationship, the more you will take out of it. One thing I remember vividly about Joe is the way he serviced his customers without thinking of what he would get out of it. When people visited his store and purchased a bottle of soda, Joe pulled out his clean white towel, meticulously wiped the ice from around the bottle, and personally handed the fresh bottle back to his customer. I may have been intimidated by Joe at age five, but the lesson stuck.

- Second, *Show Up.* I showed up at Joe's market in 1955, and good things came from it. The best two jobs I ever got were ones I showed up and walked in on without a prior appointment. In 1976, when I was searching out my first law job, I was in a high-rise building on the corner of La Brea and Hollywood Boulevard. The elevator stopped on the 10th floor. I looked past the people boarding the lift and saw the name of a law firm. I stepped out and introduced myself to the receptionist. Hey, I wanted a job with a law firm, and I thought this might be a good place. She asked: "Who are you here to see?" My response: "The hiring partner." She then proceeded to introduce me to Jim Waldorf, the hiring partner. I interviewed with Jim and secured my first job in the legal field—just by showing up.

- Third, *Follow Up.* I came back numerous times to Joe's store. I did it frequently and consistently. Joe got to know me and my siblings, and more good things happened. The bottle caps flowed, and we developed a relationship deeper than just store owner/customer. To this day, I am dedicated to following up, and doing so immediately. For example, in the summer of 2008, I followed up immediately to a meeting with Steve Wozniak, and guess what? He quickly agreed to join my Fusion-io advisory board and later worked for me as my Chief Scientist for the company. In this book, you will see that I emphasize and reemphasize the importance of *immediate* follow-up.

- Fourth, *Link Up.* Always remember we are connecting with people, and *people matter.* Some people, including my sister, thought Joe was a little tough and unapproachable. But I was so anxious to get those bottle caps that I was determined to connect with Joe despite my fear. In the end, I got my caps, and he didn't have to take out the trash.

- Fifth, *Stand Up.* In other words, be credible. Never engage in any activity either online or offline that would tarnish your reputation. Over time, as my brother and sisters and I frequented Joe's market, he became to know us as good kids from a solid family and see us as people he could trust. Joe also understood that when a five-year-old wants something badly enough, he'll be persistent enough to get it. In business, if you consistently say and do things that establish your seriousness as a player, people will take notice and respond to your requests. Be a stand-up person in every aspect of your business career so no one will ever hesitate to do business with you.

- Sixth, *Scale Up.* Building a world-class network takes hard work, time, and precise organization. You need to do something *every day* to scale up your network to make it as efficient and usable as possible. From my many visits to Joe's market in search of bottle caps, I learned that when you have a great desire for something, hard work comes naturally—because it doesn't seem like work. We spent hours collecting and organizing our bottle caps, but we didn't mind. We knew the reward would come when we played Bottle Cap Armies, so we diligently worked toward that goal. Over time, our bottle cap armies included literally thousands of bottle caps. That intimidating force was built one day at a time, one bottle cap at a time.

Throughout this book, you will see these bottle cap principles repurposed in some staggering ways. They helped me go from being the Bottle Cap Kid to the CEO of what a *BusinessWeek* Poll named the "Most Innovative Company" in the United States. They allowed me to Up My Game in ways that I never could have envisioned as a teenager sitting completely disconnected from the rest of the world in a small Montana village. Further, I will show you how you can apply those same principles in today's social media world to drive remarkable results for yourself and those around you. Networking your way to the top does take time and concerted effort, but if I can do it, so can you.

In chapter one, I begin by underscoring the importance of building relationships while you are building a network. I describe the tectonic change in networking, introduce you to the six Up Principles for successful relationship building, and describe how you can Up Your Game and become a great success in your business career through their implementation. I describe four benefits of social media networking and then suggest strategies for using technology to build your personal network.

In chapter two, I describe the importance of connecting with key people at pivotal times. I explain the power of relationships, the power of technology, and the power of relationships in changing technology. In the second half of the chapter, I explain how to develop social capital and overcome technostress.

In chapter three, I describe principle #1—Start Up. I discuss the importance of first giving to others to build relationships and explain how the law of reciprocity works to build powerful and permanent professional connections. I like to think about networking as giving with no thought of getting. Our first inclination when meeting someone should be: "How can I help this person achieve his or her big goals?" Further in the chapter, I describe how to nurture relationships with people around you so that they become mutually actionable.

Chapter four is devoted to explaining principle #2—Show Up. I initially relate a game-changing interaction which began by just showing up. I also discuss the importance of showing up online by being consistent, developing an expert craft, and creating top-of-mind awareness. In the second section, I describe the importance of showing up for people in person and how we go about making the choice to connect, creating relationship connections, and building professional chain-links. Finally, I describe how to measure the impact of your relationships.

In chapter five, principle #3—Follow Up—is explained. You will learn how to become part of an exclusive club of winners and leaders that have mastered the lost art of following up. In this chapter, I show you how to organize your network for ease, efficiency, and impact, as well as how to surpass the threshold of "Dunbar's number" by categorizing, following up immediately, and staying in touch.

In chapter six, I discuss principle #4—Link Up. Linking up with others will help you drive to the top of your profession. To Link Up is nothing more than growing and expanding the size and depth of your connections. It has several key facets—you must keep it personal, be curious about others, build win-win relationships, connect multiple times, connect on multiple platforms, transform "likes" into relationships, and build meaningful connections.

Chapter seven discusses principle #5—Stand Up. In this chapter, I discuss the importance of your reputation and focus on two important pieces of credibility: it must be earned, and it must be kept. I also discuss how to surround yourself with credibility by building a solid reputation through personal interactions and social media, choosing associations wisely, associating yourself with successful professionals, and investing in your own PR. Finally, I discuss three ways to test whether potential connections are credible and how to engage new friends responsibly.

In chapter eight, I discuss principle #6—Scale Up. There are two facets of scaling up: working smart and working hard. In the first section of the chapter, I discuss working smart by sharing the load, prioritizing your relationships, working with the end in mind, making the law of reciprocity work for you, and working smart with social media. In the second section of the chapter, I discuss how those who win and lead in business do so by working hard by giving it all they've got, building a killer team, and building successful advisory boards.

Finally, in chapter nine, I synthesize the principles, draw some final conclusions about the Up Principles, and provide powerful illustrations showing how great leaders and business colleagues have implemented these six precepts. The Up Principles will allow you to dramatically Up Your Game and win in life and relationships. Specifically, I want you to know that your relationships are your legacy. The best measure of your success is the positive influence you have in the lives of others.

I am confident that these principles will enable you to really Up Your Game. When implemented with commitment and persistence, they will be important keys to help you network your way to the top of any organization.

IT'S EASIER
THAN YOU THINK

If I told you how easy it was, you wouldn't believe me. If you asked me to strategize it, map it out, and create a campaign for it, I'd say there really isn't one. If I told you the secret was based in age-old truths simply overlaid into modern mediums, you'd wave me off with the flip of the wrist and call me "simple." The truth is . . . it's *so* simple you may not take me seriously.

The reality is that what I'm about to share with you is so very basic, you may be tempted to underestimate the very principles that could cause you to dramatically Up Your Game and make a huge difference in your career. In terms of real dollars, these principles can add potentially millions of dollars to your lifetime earnings. I'll be honest—it's so easy that those who have these principles ingrained in their nature make it look seamless, even enjoyable.

But make no mistake about it. I don't care if you are a CEO, a mid-market manager, or a college student. Anyone, including you, can develop, build, and nurture a network worth millions or even billions of dollars. I know—I did it starting from ground zero.

I'm writing this book not to entertain you or busy you. I'm writing this book because I know many of you are struggling to reinvent yourselves and your careers. The national unemployment statistics scream your pain and broadcast your discouragement. You apply to job listings and don't get the positions. You call back on hopeful leads that seem to vanish like mirages before your eyes. And you can't seem to find that open door to a future that looks bright and promising. But it doesn't have to be that hard.

Technology and networking have driven the successes of the greatest minds of this century. Leaders like Jeff Bezos, founder of Amazon and the Kindle, rose from the backburner of McDonalds as a young employee to the front pages of the *New York Times* with a revolutionary idea that would change the book industry forever. Two young college students chose a crazy name for a search engine, "Google." It is now a noun-turned-verb in conversational English as we "Google" the answers for everything.

And who can forget the legend of a man named Steve Jobs who rose, not once but twice, to the pinnacle of the technology world and brand leadership? His character and tenacity for the things he believed in were unquestioned. What possible growth in business, personal brand definition, and leadership could you experience if you mastered the use of technology combined with the fundamental principles in this book?

A tectonic change in networking, facilitated by online social media, has enabled individuals and businesses to connect with people like never before. The benefits to social media networking are many, but social media must be used in conjunction with six classic "old-school" principles to be effective. With the framework and tips I provide here, you'll be on your way to succeeding as a leader and winning in business and life.

The Tectonic Change in Networking

Networking, simply stated, is doing everything you can on a regular basis to secure and expand your personal relationships in order to increase the likelihood for success—your own success and the success of others. I would also define networking as developing an extended group of people with similar interests or concerns that interact and remain in contact for mutual support and assistance. Through the benefits of technology, your networking reach can be wider and deeper than ever before.

In 2009, while serving as CEO of Fusion-io, I was in New York City meeting with the lifeblood of our business—our customers. There, I met a fascinating guy—Hylton Van Zyl, one of the heads of Research and Development for Credit-Suisse, one of the top financial institutions in the world. He was kind enough to share his business card with me.

Having only met Hylton one time, it would have been easy to tuck the business card away and forget about it. Our interaction could have been left to a handshake and a "Hylton, it was nice meeting you." But, instead, when I returned home from that trip, I logged his contact information in my database and reached out to follow up with him. I extended a LinkedIn invitation, and Hylton became a contact for me in the New York City area.

Three years later, in March of 2012, as I was looking to grow HireVue, I sent out a LinkedIn blast to what were then my 196 direct contacts in the New York City area. Hylton Van Zyl responded. He introduced me to Neill Ochiogrosso with Investor Growth Capital in New York. I followed up with a note to Neill, and a meeting was arranged. The introduction turned into a stellar connection. A couple of days later, I found myself seated in a big conference room with a number of partners and associates of IGC. As our meeting was reaching completion, Neill turned to me with an enthusiastic grin and said, "David, this is right down the middle of our fairway." Stated another way, HireVue was at the size and historical point in its development as a company where his group liked to invest. We'd talked a little about golf, and the analogy was fitting. Through that simple connection, we were able to raise a total of 22 million dollars.

The moral of the story is this: Business is all about connecting. The more you connect, the more efficiently you connect; and the more credibly you connect, the more success you will have. Social media networking enables people to connect more efficiently and cost effectively than ever before.

Four Benefits of Social Media Networking

Social media has shifted the way people make, build, and nurture relationships. It gives you incredible new powers to create new business opportunities and connections for yourself and your company. Stated another way, it can be a game changer for you where properly applied. When you consider the various ways that you can optimize your opportunities and improve the trajectory of your business career, giving you an ability to truly Up Your Game, the tools of today's social media can be amazingly impactful. Social media has four main benefits: it's free, it's time-efficient, it's effective, and it's edifying.

Free

Perhaps one of the greatest benefits of using a massive personal social network to solve challenging issues is that *it's free*. There is no need to hire a set of consultants or engage with a third-party company that charges for these crowdsourcing services. Your personal outsourcing is absolutely free—and much more efficacious, because you will often know the source from which a given recommendation is made. Anyone who has developed a reputation for credibility and service is capable of reaching out to hundreds, if not thousands, of people to obtain a variety of fresh ideas and solutions to help them solve their day-to-day tasks. One example is the talent search. A savvy social media networker can save a company hundreds of thousands of dollars by reaching out directly to individuals rather than a recruitment firm. Recently, I know of a company that spent $150,000 in fees using a third-party firm to recruit their VP of Sales. They also gave up some equity in their company. At Fusion-io, I simply blasted a LinkedIn message to thousands of folks and was able to identify and hire the world's best VP of sales in the data storage marketplace. Further, with the very specific use of social media, I went on to hire a game-changing CFO, as well as one of the best executive assistants on the planet.

Time-Efficient

When I had an issue that needed resolution, I used to walk down the hall of my office and consult with colleagues to seek their advice. Whether my need was how to handle a potential legal matter, how to deal with a particular personnel issue, or how to find a new employee to fill a critical role in the organization, I spent time chatting about the concern and asking questions of my office colleagues to find a solution. But this old-school method of corporate problem solving was time intensive and limited in perspective—there were, after all, only a few people at that water cooler.

Today, there is a revolutionary way of getting things done and finding solutions—brought to us courtesy of social media. Going to lunch with Bob may be easy and comfortable, but it is incredibly inefficient in terms of getting answers to burning questions at the office. So while your lunch with Bob or Mary or Sally or Joe may be useful to deepen a relationship, there are more effective ways of reaching out with today's twenty-first-century tools of communication. Instead, you can seek the knowledge of the *masses* to quickly and efficiently help you further your success in business with smart use of social media.

The benefit of calling upon people in a single moment of time to help solve a business issue is analogous to solving the problem of a slow computer hard drive with solid-state storage solution. A task that used to take a company seven hours to achieve can now be accomplished in three minutes through the implementation of solid-state technologies. For example, hiring a VP of marketing might take you days, if not weeks, to achieve if you asked one or two personal colleagues at the water cooler for recommendations. It can now be achieved in a matter of hours—if not minutes.

People wonder all the time at my capacity to get so many things done seemingly simultaneously. Let me tell you my dirty little secret: I don't have just one or two friends helping me solve my business issues. *I have thousands of them!*

Effective

Through social media networking, I am able to effectively uncover the people who have specific expertise on any issue I may be confronting. I don't rely on old-school luck that a colleague in the adjacent office will have the perfect solution. I do this by blasting questions, by categorizing, and by microtargeting.

Let me explain how this works. Quite simply, I frame my question to thousands of Internet connections and try to obtain the best possible result. For example, if I am looking for a Sr. VP of Marketing with digital media experience, I can post a Facebook message to my 5000 Facebook friends that asks simply: "Who is the best marketing person you know in matters related to digital media?" In a matter of minutes, I will instantly have qualified resources offered through responding posts and emails.

Sometimes, I have a specific question that I need to pose to select individuals rather than an entire group. For this, I use a dynamic Facebook tool—categories. I have categorized all of my 5000 Facebook friends into roughly 50 categories. The same is true with my email accounts. LinkedIn even provides a built-in categorization system to allow you to hone in on people with specific backgrounds, such as real estate agents, venture capitalists, accountants, lawyers, and so on.

One of the personal categories I use to organize my connections on my email accounts and on Facebook is "Marketing and PR." Approximately 350 of my Facebook friends have backgrounds in this area. How do I know? Whenever I add a new Facebook friend, I religiously, and almost obsessively, study that person's background and interests by perusing his or her profile. I, then, place that person into the appropriate lists or categories. So, when I am ready to find that VP of Marketing, I can quickly access my list of marketing contacts from my Facebook database and seek advice, ask for references, or pursue one of my Facebook friends as a possible candidate.

On LinkedIn, I have more than five million contacts that are only one degree of separation from me. In fact, using LinkedIn, I have the power to contact over 30 million people directly or through a connection. This allows me to search, as I frequently do, for qualified resources to find expertise in Information Technology, Computer Hardware, Software, Telecommunications, and Wireless Markets, among others. This gives me a thousand times better results than asking Bob at the water cooler.

Microtargeting is also a useful tool. LinkedIn allows me to send messages based on job title, location, size of company, or industry. There are roughly 150 industries that can be targeted separately. As of April 2014, I have nearly 12,000 people with whom I am directly connected on LinkedIn with another 17,000 on Facebook, Yahoo, and Google+, totaling over 25,000 connections. They are located in 76 countries around the globe. 429 are business owners, 333 are CEOs, and 306 are presidents of companies. I know them by location, as well: I have 2600 contacts in the Salt Lake City area, over 1600 in the San Francisco Bay Area, 550 plus in Orange County, California, 405 in New York City,

400 plus in Los Angeles, and another 265 in Washington, DC. I also categorize them by company: 71 work at Microsoft, 58 at Google, 48 at Oracle, and 44 at IBM.

Let me share a real-life example. Several years ago, I was raising money for the Checketts Global Sports Fund, a $250 million fund whose investors own parts of professional sports franchises. I needed to quickly and effectively target high net worth investors. I targeted these relevant categories within LinkedIn: Banking, Broadcast Media (the fund had a strong focus on media rights associated with sporting events), Capital Markets, Entertainment, Executive Officers, Fundraising, Investment Banking, Recreational Facilities and Management, Sports, Venture Capital, and Private Equity. I blasted out an email to those targeted categories and successfully connected with millions of potential dollars in investment and set up fourteen key meetings in just a matter of hours. Clearly, social media networking can increase your effectiveness through blasting questions, categorizing, and microtargeting.

Edifying

A large percentage of the people to whom I might pose a problem are friends and acquaintances. In most instances, I already know the background or expertise of a particular individual who responds to my call for help. It is a beautiful thing to find solutions to numerous everyday business problems simply by tapping into my database of connections across the globe. I find it fulfilling to collaborate with and supply answers to time-sensitive questions in an efficient manner. I recall on one occasion I was asked to set up a series of meetings in the Silicon Valley for a start-up company seeking venture capital financing. Within one day, I had set up eleven meetings for this company. The CEO was beside himself with appreciation, and I must say I got a kick out of it, as well. That was exhilarating and edifying.

There are many reasons people actively engage with me in seeking, for example, a key hire for their company. One reason is that they inherently understand the *law of reciprocity*. That is, they intuitively know that since they have helped me in the past with one of my business challenges, they know I will reciprocate.

There is a hidden benefit to all of this social networking. As you reach out to others to ask questions and seek their opinions and assistance, you establish yourself as a credible source—someone who is "in the know," someone who is current, and someone who is open to sharing knowledge. When you help people with their needs, you establish yourself as someone who has a positive, "can-do" attitude and is capable of providing a reciprocal act of service. Your ability to incorporate the power of mass collaboration in solving business issues is directly proportional to the degree that you have helped others in the past and the degree that you are seen as someone with credibility.

To summarize, utilizing social media is a powerful way to connect because...

It's free. You can now take advantage of the network you've built over time with your own sweat equity. Recognize the incremental value of adding even just one person of interest to your network so you can obtain thoughts, resources, and advice from hundreds of contacts—not just a handful.

It's time-efficient. Benjamin Franklin once said, "Dost thou love life? Then do not squander the stuff life is made of." I believe he was referring to *time*. I can send a LinkedIn message to 200 of my closest colleagues in less than two minutes. I can post a Facebook message in less than 30 seconds that will be seen by 5,000 Facebook friends. Use your time and relationships wisely!

It's effective. Connect with people who are specialists in a given area or expertise. People who typically respond to a broad-based message will most likely do so if they have value to add. While it is true that you may also have a random comment or post, that is a small price to pay for the benefit you gain from the efficiency, depth, and diversity of skill sets you obtain by seeking the expertise of crowdsourcing. Your ability to get the right answer in the shortest amount of time and resolve your problems increases exponentially when you connect to the masses directly and personally.

It's edifying. You become established as someone "in the know," someone who is making things happen. You can generate a buzz and an interest for your projects and your company. Many people comment daily, thanking me and saying, "I love your quotes on Facebook," or "Thank you for that LinkedIn message," or "I learned from that discussion thread." Your ability to connect, inform, inspire, and promote edifies others and yourself, your projects, and your business.

You have to build this network not just through technology, but also through time-honored principles that make the difference between having a presence on social media platforms and actually engaging in a real way with people using social media.

Many people talk about being "experts in social media." They can describe in great detail methods of setting up fan pages on Facebook, using groups on LinkedIn, tweeting strategically, and setting up a blog that integrates social media. These experts emphasize the "media" in social media—but they should be emphasizing the "social," because that personal engagement is something that cannot be replaced. I know only a very small number of people who actually leverage the power of "social" media to succeed in their endeavors or solve their business problems. These are the people who intrinsically understand the six basic principles of effective networking that will be discussed in this book.

Remember this important point: These social media tools are only methods of connecting with people. It is the people that matter, not the tools. So while twenty-first century social media tools like Twitter, Google+, Facebook, Instagram, and LinkedIn are useful, the real objective should be the implementation of the underlying six principles of building, lasting relationships in order to Up Your Game.

Six Principles to Up Your Game

In my career, I have implemented six fundamental principles to build relationships and grow businesses. The steps seemed natural to me. They came easily based on my love for and curiosity about people. Nobody spoon-fed me the insights or made charts or graphs that explained the concepts. The business and relationship successes I have had seemed part of the passion and zeal I had internally. But I have also seen many others who consciously cultivated these skill sets. Bill Gates, for example, is not a naturally gregarious networker of people, but through key professional relationships which he built, he acquired DOS and went on to do a deal with IBM worth arguably more than $100 billion over time. Ray Noorda, the man who built Novell into a company that Bill Gates tried to buy for ten billion dollars, was not outgoing in any way. And yet he became known as the king of indirect sales channels and business partnerships. Steve Jobs was much more outgoing than Bill or Ray, but even he had to learn over time the importance of relationship building. To me, business is all about connections.

I believe the adage, "You are the average of the five people you surround yourself with." So, I have always tried to collaborate with people with exceptional skills, thereby increasing my own IQ. I realized early on in my career that a passion for working with people demands *intuitive, internal* personal work, not superficial lip service. These are things that one cultivates in his or her character *intentionally*. They can neither be purchased nor sold.

The following six principles can be cultivated and harvested. Every great leader with whom I have worked has demonstrated one or more of these precepts in a powerful way. Each principle, applied independently, can create massive results in your business and personal life. Combined, they can bring exponential personal growth and business success.

1. **Start Up.** The first step in building any permanent, actionable personal network is to give with no thought of getting. Networking needs to start well before you need something. At its core, networking is more about giving than taking. Arthur Ashe once said: "From what we get we make a living; from what we give however, we make a life"—and, I might add, a network.

2. **Show Up.** Be there in person, and be there online.

3. **Follow Up.** Immediate follow up is absolutely essential to stay top of mind. Stay in touch. Be memorable.

4. **Link Up.** In the end, we are linking with people—and people matter. When connecting with people, make everything personal.

5. **Stand Up.** Be a credible, stand-up person. Never engage in any activity that would give people pause in terms of working with or recommending you.

6. **Scale Up.** Building a world-class network takes hard work and time. With each passing day, one needs to do something to build, monitor, and expand the network.

It surprises me to find how easily individuals will adapt to new technology yet struggle with building and maintaining deep personal relationships. Today there are over 2.5 billion users of the web, versus 16 million in 1995. Yet, how many of those users know the value of the time spent online, the significance of Facebook relationships, the power of LinkedIn, or the connecting capabilities of Twitter and Instagram? Even more significantly, how many know the importance of their integrity and personal brand while using it?

There is tremendous power behind the mouse when a person can combine character and relationships *with* technology. It is this ability (and one you can develop, too) that has helped me create, build, sustain, and nurture deep relationships with such widely dispersed people as the inventor of the Apple computer, an NFL Hall of Famer, the man who took Google to a half trillion in value, and a man who came within a whisker of being the President of the United States in 2012.

Can I share what I've learned to help you succeed, as well? The possibilities are endless when you harness the tools that compel the masses. While the principles themselves are timeless, the marriage of principle and application create the synergy that we often see as an "overnight" success. That missing link is what I believe many of you in business are hungering for but are somehow missing. If you want to massively increase your chances for success and step Up Your Game, use these twenty-first century tools together with the underlying six principles.

Networking effectively allowed me to help build a billion-dollar valuation for a company that had been shipping product for less than three years. Through simple, clear steps that I will teach you, my database has grown deep and wide enough to create a massive pool of talent and intellect for me to tap into to grow boards of directors, find capital, and bring leadership. I will share with you the keys to finding, tracking, and sourcing the best possible talent for your team.

In the remainder of this book, I will delve into the Up Principles and show you how to apply them to this brave new world of digital communication and social interaction. On our journey, I will demonstrate how giving with no thought of getting, credibility, and simple email communications helped attract Steve Wozniak, the inventor of the Apple computer, to join one of my companies; how I hired the best CFO on the planet using Facebook while remembering that people matter; and how, with LinkedIn, I attracted one of the top sales VP's in the world by simply "following up and staying in touch"—a hire that helped to change the destiny of a company.

Final Tips

In 2011, my wife, Linda, and I were out to dinner with the CEO of Attachmate, Jeff Hawn. As the dinner went on, the subject of networking came up in the discussion. Jeff was interested in finding people to add to his newly acquired company, Novell. Linda turned to Jeff and said, "Hey, my husband can help you! He is the Human Internet." That nickname has stuck. I connect people because I see the benefit and, frankly, the joy it has brought to me personally and the companies with which I have been associated. It benefits my friends and acquaintances. It benefits the products to be formulated, developed, and sold. It benefits the customer. If I can teach you how to do this and why, your network will grow. Then you, too, will begin to see that it *is* easy.

Networking is an opportunity, not a nuisance. In a regular day, you'll meet between one and five new people. How many of those new acquaintances are now connected with you on some social media platform? Are they Twitter followers, Facebook friends, Instagram followers, or LinkedIn connections? If not, then why not? If you are not taking full advantage of the horsepower of Facebook, Twitter, Google+, and Linkedin, you have—at minimum—a competitive disadvantage in the marketplace. I built up a large personal network of 10,000 plus connections on LinkedIn, 5000 Facebook friends, and nearly 25,000 email contacts while running several multimillion-dollar companies through one simple guiding principle—Do it every day!

CHAPTER 1 GAME PLAN

Here are some tips to jumpstart your own network and accelerate your move to the top. These are immediately implementable and will rapidly infuse your network with new vitality and direction. Harness these methods of twenty-first century communication, and watch your networking influence grow and your career take off.

1. Stay in touch with people you like and respect, even if they can't help you immediately. Be willing to do something for them—something out of the ordinary, something they will remember you by, such as sharing with them a newspaper article or small gift, etc. You don't want to access people only when you are desperate. Make this part of a drip campaign, and watch your effective database grow.

2. Talk to people everywhere you go. Weddings, parties, and soccer games are just the beginning. Don't forget about airplane rides, church, the supermarket line, sporting events, festivals, dance recitals, concerts, bookstores, and so forth. Each is an opportunity to meet a new contact, a new resource, or a new specialist.

3. Learn to ask the question, "What do you do?" Or, my personal favorite, "What is your story?" Ask people about their background, their skills, and their life circumstances with genuine interest. Become curious.

4. Keep a business card or fabulous-looking updated brochure or other form of information about yourself on you at all times. Get comfortable handing out your card. More importantly, collect business cards from others. Once you have the other person's

CHAPTER 1 GAME PLAN

contact information, it puts you in control. When you return from an event, don't count the number of cards you handed out—count the number of cards you collected.

5. Join every networking club and association in your field, whether in the physical world or online. Join Instagram, LinkedIn, FourSquare, Facebook, Twitter, Pinterest, Google+, and other up-and-coming social media platforms.

6. Follow up on any contacts. Do it that very night. I make it a practice to follow up with every single individual I meet with an email message, LinkedIn invitation, or Facebook request within 24 hours of an event. Immediacy of follow-up is a lost art. It is a hidden competitive advantage. Do it.

The reality of today's leadership demands individuals who will step up and connect with others. It demands people who will develop deep and trusting relationships. It demands people who will network. It demands problem solvers. In the pages and chapters that follow, you and I will bridge the gaps that keep you from the door of opportunity. These gaps may be logical, relational, or emotional. That door, that "parting of the clouds," that "perfect contact" may be one click away, my friend. Flex those Rolodex fingers, take a deep breath, and let's get started.

TIMELESS PRINCIPLES, CHANGING TECHNOLOGY

During the summer of my sixteenth year, I wrote my first novel about a Viking ship marooned on a desert island. Seated in my father's Yellowstone shop on the main street of Red Lodge, Montana, I had plenty of opportunity to daydream and to write. When business was slow and the visions would come, I would grab my yellow pad and lead pencil and get lost in the adventures of Captain Smith and his nefarious crew. I've since lost the manuscript to my epic adventure, but my passion for writing—ignited by my English teacher, Audrey Bailey—has remained. Mrs. Bailey inspired me to improve my skills, use my imagination, believe in myself, and find a format for self-expression. Many years later, I still feel her influence when I sit down to write.

We have all been impacted, compelled, inspired, and challenged by significant people at important times in our lives.

Reciprocally, it is also true that you have the potential to impact others tremendously in their pivotal moments. You may never know when your words encourage growth, how your resources have lifted another's burdens, or what your actions have put into motion. This is the greatest wisdom I have to offer you: *Nothing will define you more than the people who impact your life at pivotal junctures.*

Relationships are powerful, whether they are developed through solid interpersonal relationships or ever-changing technology. Technology, if properly applied, can be used to strengthen those relationships and exponentially increase your reach and influence. But, if improperly applied, technology can hurt your chances for success. Learning to increase your social capital and overcoming technostress will allow you to secure deep, personal connections that become actionable in your life and help you Up Your Game.

Relationship Power

Just like my sixteen-year-old self, I find great satisfaction in expressing myself, connecting thoughts and people, and generating ideas. I am still compelled by words, information, creativity, and imagination. How grateful I am for a teacher that took the time to encourage me to stretch myself. Today, I realize more than ever the impact one person can make on another; and today, instead of a yellow notepad and pencil as the vehicle for my ideas, I pound away on an Apple laptop signed in permanent marker by my friend Steve Wozniak—someone who was also greatly influenced by a teacher.

Steve Wozniak, the computer scientist who built the first Apple computer, struggled like all of us to find his identity. But he did know that he was good at math. When he was in third grade, there was an important math contest held at his school. Steve won. As he walked out of school that day, his beaming teacher grabbed him by the shoulders and said, "Steve, you are a math genius!"

Steve went home and promptly told his mom, "I'm a math genius!" That self-affirmation was self-fulfilling—it perpetuated his decisions, fueled his drive, and ultimately made him one of the greatest scientists in the history of America. His teacher's personal encouragement, at that pivotal moment in his life, indirectly propelled one of the greatest technological developments of the twentieth century.

Our time on Earth plays out as a series of connections that move us through our lives based on who we know and how we interact with them. Our relationships are a priceless commodity. They, more than any other factor, determine the road map we take from one stage in our lives to another. Often it is one relationship, one chance meeting, one person of impact, or one simple conversation that opens the next door to the fulfilling of our dreams and aspirations. It will be your relationships that determine your ability to lead and succeed in your chosen profession.

Floppy Disks and Facebook and How They Impact Relationships

The basic purpose of many of the technologies of the last forty years, from floppy disks to flash drives to Facebook, is to store, share, and assimilate information. For centuries, philosophers and scientists have been collecting, storing, and sharing information through oral tradition, illuminated manuscripts, and costly printing presses. We now have the luxury of tapping a screen on our iPhone or Kindle Fire. Within seconds, our soul's genius is stored and then propagated to reach thousands.

Assimilating information and building relationships can work together to synergistically open doors. But doors are often closed to those without key personal or professional connections. Sometimes it takes someone to shove open the door. Let me share with you the following experience that taught me, the hard way, the value of being connected and the need, at times, to push open our own doors to opportunity. As a young law student at Brigham Young University in the winter of 1975, I was anxious to locate a placement for my summer clerkship. Summer positions are incredibly important to law students—if a student does well, the internship may become a permanent position after graduation. I was often told that one's ability to get a summer clerkship with a good firm was dependent upon grades. I worked hard to do well academically while maintaining a side job flipping burgers at BYU's Cougareat to support my small family. As it turned out, grades were only a small portion of the formula. The real key to securing a summer clerkship was connections. So despite my excellent grades, I was shocked to discover that many of my peers had clerkships lined up after their second year of law school. *I was not one of them.*

The burden of getting a placement and providing for my family was overwhelming. At the time, Linda and I were the proud parents of two children and were expecting a third. During Christmas break, I found myself commiserating with my mother, Kay, about my predicament. As I shared my anxiety with my wonderful mother, she looked at me and said, "David, haven't I explained to you that, in life, it is not *what* you know but *who* you know?" From that point on, I realized that I had the ability to build relationships, and those relationships would build me.

My father, while blessed with an enthusiasm for life and a winning personality, was not a connector. I had come from a small town, but if there was a lawyer in that town, I did not know him. I had zero connections in the legal world. Nevertheless, I was determined to secure a clerkship *somewhere*. My ultimate dream was to secure a clerkship in sunny California. Linda had grown up in Southern California, and the first ten years of my life were spent in Burbank. The fact that I did not know one lawyer in the California market was intimidating. Driven, however, by desperation and concern to provide for my family, I was laser focused on finding something there. I found a publication that listed all of the law firms in California and targeted one hundred firms. My wonderful wife and I plunked away on the typewriter until we'd created a resume and a cover letter. Despite concerns over the cost of postage stamps and carbon copy paper, we proceeded to flood the L.A. market with pleas for a job. Number of responses: 3.

I felt like I was the least connected guy in the universe. How I wished I could have had the relationship capital to write a letter that would receive numerous responses from people interested in what I had to offer. Sadly, I knew no one. My letters were basically paper cold calls. I was committed to the cause, but I was discouraged. But I did have three leads.

We eventually jumped in our car (with a rebuilt engine, I might add, because our car had blown up on our honeymoon) and visited each of those three law firms. One was based in the heart of Hollywood, California, across the street from the Grauman's (now TCL) Chinese theater at the corner of La Brea and Hollywood Boulevard. Within the first few minutes of the interview, it was apparent that they were hiring exclusively from the top California law schools like Stanford, UC Berkeley, or UCLA. My chances were not good. Leaving the interview feeling discouraged, I stepped into the elevator.

I felt depleted—desperation and frustration were starting to get the best of me. I felt overwhelmed and doubted my abilities. I felt like quitting. But I shook off the feeling, stayed alert, and watched for an opportunity to connect.

As the elevator stopped on the 10th floor, I happened to glance up. The name on the reception desk just outside the elevator read, "Law Offices of Irsfeld, Irsfeld, and Younger." I took a deep breath and stepped out of the elevator. I walked to the receptionist and stated, "I am here to see the hiring partner for the law firm."

The receptionist replied warmly, "I'll go see if Mr. Waldorf is in." A few minutes later, Jim Waldorf appeared, and I was offered a clerkship for the summer of 1976.

Irsfeld, Irsfeld, and Younger became the point of ignition for my entire career. But getting that initial position had been incredibly difficult because I had zero connections to individual practitioners of the law. I had not known a single lawyer in Southern California. Not one single lawyer in Southern California had known me. That is, until the day that I collected their information, showed up, and got connected.

Success happens through the impact of specific people at a pivotal time. Our lives are a series of connections—each one is another chapter in that journey. What information are you storing and sharing? How is it connecting you to others? How are those connections being used to create a long-term game plan for success and leadership?

As I point out elsewhere in this book, although I have been in the computer industry in some way, shape, or form for 30 plus years, my educational background is not in tech. In fact, the one computer science course I tried to take in college, I walked out of after the first day. Frankly, at my age, things like texting, hashtags, Google+, tagging, etc., scare me. But I also realized if I wanted to stay relevant and part of today's technology conversation, then it was essential that I continue to dive in like I did that day in 1976 to secure my first law job. You have to show up and be seen in tech circles from Facebook to Instagram to SnapChat to LinkedIn and beyond.

My wife is a huge inspiration to me on this point. At the age of 55, she went back to college and spent five years working to obtain her Ph.D. She succeeded marvelously and received her doctorate in Instructional Psychology and Technology. If you think it is easy, in your late 50's, to take a complex course in statistics, think again. Now that's intimidating. But Linda dove in and succeeded. As a result, she and her company, the VIEW—Virtual Immersive Educational World—are on the cusp of changing how higher education and training are delivered to the world.

Top-of-Mind Awareness

Back when my wife and I were copying, folding, and stuffing envelopes with my resume and cover letter, I did not understand "top-of-mind awareness" as I do today. "Top-of-mind awareness" is making yourself or your product recognizably present in the minds of your audience. Just as advertising agencies create top-of-mind awareness with brand names, logos, and jingles, you can create top-of-mind awareness by nurturing deep relationships—even when doing so does not come easily or naturally to you.

Some years ago, Fram oil filter aired a commercial for its product. The commercial opens with an image of a stalling car and a very frustrated driver. The mechanic smartly states, "Pay me now or pay me later." The commercial suggested that the customer should pay the small price of the oil filter to avoid a large bill following an emergency.

The same concept holds true in relationships. Either you take the time to build deep, healthy, growing friendships and connections now, or you will be forced to build them under duress as your possibilities become limited at some future point in time. My advice? Grow them now. Create your own top-of-mind awareness in the minds of groups of people who can and will support you through changes and circumstances you cannot foresee today. Build them this week. Network today.

In the fall of 2010, I was playing golf in the small, Southern Utah city of St. George. When time permits, as it did that day, I enjoy dropping into a golf course randomly and going out as a single player. Typically, the pro shop will pair you with someone, which was true that day. It was relaxing, picturesque, and enjoyable—great downtime to regroup and renew. But if I'd had a "downtime" mentality that day, then I would have missed a tremendous opportunity for the company of which I was CEO at the time: Fusion-io.

As we were approaching the 17th tee, one of my fellow competitors remarked, "See that home off the 18th fairway? That home belongs to the former governor of the state of Utah, Mike Leavitt." I looked to see the house to which he referred. As it turns out, I knew Mike and his wife, Jackie. Mike was a member of the Fusion-io advisory board, whom I had invited when he left the government service as Secretary of Health and Human Services. I made a mental note to swing by their home when I finished my round of golf.

About 30 minutes later, I found myself wandering through the Coral Canyon housing development trying to identify the house pointed out earlier by my golf companion. When I'd located it, I walked up to the door and knocked. Much to my disappointment, no one answered. As I was returning to my car, I thought to myself that I should leave a note for Mike and Jackie letting them know I had been in the area and had stopped by to say "hello." I could not find a piece of paper to write on. After standing there for a moment, I remembered I had some Fusion-io business cards in my golf bag. I opened my trunk and took a moment to write a greeting.

Tucking my personalized card into the crack of the front door, I heard a car drive up. Much to my surprise, it was Jackie Leavitt and Mike's assistant. We had a great chat as we stood outside their home. Jackie explained that this was the first time they had been to their home in southern Utah for more than six months. It was a major coincidence that I happened to swing by on that particular day. (Albert Einstein once said that "coincidences are God's way of remaining anonymous.")

I asked if I could carry in their groceries, and that gave me the opportunity to learn more about the Leavitts and the construction of their beautiful home. Jackie and I enjoyed an animated discussion. Then she stopped and said, "Hey, we are having our annual Christmas party here in a couple of weeks. Would you and your wife like to come?"

Several weeks later, Linda and I returned to St. George and attended Mike and Jackie's Christmas party. It was a fabulous event with incredible people and festivities. While there, I met Randy Fields. Randy had been married to Debbie Fields, the founder of Mrs. Fields Cookies. Randy had his own software company in Park City, Utah, called the Park City Group. As I shared my work with Fusion-io, Randy became very excited about what we did. He expressed a strong interest in testing our technology to help his business. Later that evening, following the event, I sent an email to my new friend Randy introducing him to Fusion-io's Trent Richards. Trent was our sales executive for that region. As it turned out, Randy's company was in need of Fusion-io's technology, and a significant sale ensued.

There are many lessons to be derived from this relatively simple occurrence. First, never take downtime from networking and connecting. This can happen anywhere, anytime. It happens naturally and effortlessly by engaging with people and caring about their needs. Second, take action. Drop in on an old friend. Pack business cards in your golf bag. Listen to strangers. Help take in the groceries. Third, follow up. Timing is essential. Follow up immediately when you meet someone, when they express a need, when you know someone or something that could support their success. You never know how that can impact their situation.

Did I mention how grateful my sales rep was for this seemingly coincidental encounter? His email said it all: "The hottest thing you have sent over lately is Randy Fields at the Park City Group. They just purchased a couple of 1.28 TB cards. You have a knack for selling more Fusion-io at a dinner party than I get done in a week of pounding the phones. Keep them coming. Trent."

Networking is an investment, not a nuisance. Every time you come across a person or an activity that impresses you, make a mental and physical note to do something about it. When you keep yourself top of mind, the universe conspires to make things happen for you and will allow you to forge your way to the top.

Technology Power

Technology, used well, can build and nurture relationships. While deep, personal relationships are always most effectively nurtured in person, technology can enhance your ability to develop relationships. But used poorly, or without wisdom and discretion, technology can destroy relationships and reputations. When using technology to network, make sure to develop your profile deliberately, share cautiously, and think long term.

Develop Your Profile Deliberately

Established with deliberate thought and written well with concise verbiage and quoted references, a LinkedIn profile can open doors to prospective employers, joint ventures, and strategic network alliances. The same can be said with Facebook. I have actually determined not to interview someone based on the nature of things I have seen on individual Facebook feeds. As I peruse Instagram, as well, I find myself thinking: "Gee, based on that photo, I would never hire that person." Further to that point, any social media profile that sits unedited, incomplete, or with inaccurate information is very damaging.

Technology is your first impression on those in your periphery. Prospective clients may determine to move closer or farther away based on what they see or don't see. Employ discretion when choosing your photographic images, your verbiage, and your letters of reference. Determine how to feature your assets to display them best in whatever medium you choose, whether it is LinkedIn, Foursquare, Facebook, Twitter, or Pinterest. People are watching, and they will make decisions on how you represent yourself.

Share Cautiously

Share cautiously. This is more important than ever with the relaxed platforms of Facebook, SnapChat, and Instagram. The creator of Facebook himself has said, "People have really gotten comfortable not only sharing more information and different kinds, but more openly and with more people—and that social norm is just something that has evolved over time." It is not uncommon to see risqué pictures, details of a highly charged run-in at the gas station, or even comments about a former spouse in people's Facebook posts shared with the world. While it is common to see these things, I encourage people to avoid being "common." Choose to share information about your personal life that would inspire or connect to people, but refrain from posting things that degrade character or offend others.

Twitter, for example, is a powerful medium that shouts your immediate thoughts and impressions. Be careful! Just like an important email should be read and reviewed with caution before pressing the "send" button, Twitter posts must be filtered and tempered. It has become commonplace to hear the fallout in the media of celebrity rants posted on Twitter. Unfortunately, it is hard to repair reputations that are damaged by a thoughtless, random tweet. There are now hundreds of cases of those who have tweeted casual thoughts only to issue a retraction or apology later.

On the other hand, an insightful communication on LinkedIn, Facebook, or Twitter, can have a marvelously positive impact on your job prospects. The other day, I received a very well-written LinkedIn message from a senior in college. I was so impressed that I immediately wrote this young lady back asking her what her plans beyond graduation were. On another occasion, I hired an intern at HireVue based on a smart Facebook communication received from this individual.

Choose the content that you share wisely so your Internet relationships and personal profiles match the life you lead offline, as well.

Think Long Term

In school, a large portion of our elementary and high school researching was done with heavy books at the library. In these monstrous editions, we would search for individuals, wars, countries, and government statistics. Today, research is done online through Google, Wikipedia, Ask.com, and a host of online academic databases. Whatever people read on the Internet, they believe to be true—especially if the ranking is high and the information goes viral. I am aware of too many situations where a rogue employee does something dumb and puts the entire company at risk, exposing both the employee and the company to something known as "Google death."

With the implementation of the Facebook Timeline and the location tracker from Foursquare, anyone, friend or foe, can piece together your online data and have a running history of your relationships, jobs, former locations and homes, restaurants you've frequented, and stores you've visited. Your history is laid out before the world with much more detail than you probably realize. This history can have serious consequences, personally and professionally.

People who know you (as well as people who almost know you and people who are thinking about knowing you) will make decisions based on your social media history, right or wrong. Opportunities for connections, job possibilities, and joint ventures will depend heavily on information amassed online. People will invest emotionally in a relationship with you because they believe in your character. Robert K. Cooper, author of *The Other 90%*, said it best: "People won't put their hearts into something they don't believe in. They might put their intellect into it, but not their hearts."

To up your networking game, take a page from Socrates' playbook and "know thyself." Build your profile deliberately, share cautiously, and think long term as you build an online presence that accurately reflects who you are and who you want to become. Know thy profile, thy online history, thy timeline, and thy Google presence. All of those things together will build a lasting impression and help you as a leader in your profession.

Where Will You Be in Five Years?

Today, a floppy disk is as relevant and useful as an 8-track tape. "What is an 8-track tape?" you ask. My point, exactly. Technology will continue to evolve. As Bill Gates said, "We always overestimate the change that will occur in the next two years and underestimate the change that will occur in the next ten." If you want to expand your network, then find the most forward-thinking technologies and use them to promote your best assets and skills and connect with others who can be resources to you. Remember, however, that technology is *only* the vehicle for information. To create lasting relationships, you need to overcome technostress and develop social capital.

Overcome "Technostress"

Some of you reading this book remember when snail mail was the main method of transportation for ideas. Others who are reading this book have no clue what "D.O.S." means and have never played the Atari game, "Pong." If you are one of these people, I want to stop and address something that may have large segments of you already hyperventilating. This is the concept of "technostress." A phrase coined by Dr. Larry Rosen and Dr. Michelle Weil, "technostress" is the anxiety people feel when faced with changing technology. As we're forced to adapt to changing technology, we are also forced to face our learning blocks and our self-confidence issues. Inviting you to tackle networking and technology together may feel like a one-two punch from a cyber demon. But technostress can be overcome if you go at your own speed, share meaningful information, and become educated.

Go at Your Own Speed

I am anything but a techno-geek. I don't have a degree in computer science, and I've never taken a course in engineering. So if I have mastered these technological platforms, you can too! Let me speak truthfully: These skills are not learned overnight. But they can be learned. They aren't learned in a crash course, but they can be memorized and implemented over time. If the new Facebook timeline scares you, pick up the telephone and connect with people old-school style. If you feel a panic attack coming on just thinking about your first tweet, write a handwritten thank-you card, instead. There is no right method—only a beginning. No need to be judged, cajoled, pushed, or manipulated. Go at your own speed, but go!

Share Something Meaningful

The greatest fuel is to believe you have something of worth to share with others—even if that "something" is good old-fashioned friendship. Do not underestimate how powerful this is. Many people today feel isolated, stressed, anxious, and depressed in their day-to-day lives. A simple "hello" or visit is welcomed and appreciated. For some, it is the connection that keeps them going in their busy day and the support and validation that inspires them to keep working toward their goals. Never underestimate your ability to build others through simple conversation. Keep your focus there, and implement the technology that supports your message.

Comedian George Carlin said, "Electricity is really just organized lightning." Technology and social media are the same—a method of organizing relationship electricity. Do not be scared if one method of organizing or management doesn't fit for you. Find a method that fits your style, your personality, and your relationships.

Become Educated

If you don't know how to use these technological platforms for relationship building, there are several ways to become educated.

Learn from the Web. First, let the Web teach you for free. You have unlimited learning at the tips of your fingers. If you want to learn a program or a social media platform, there are easily twenty free videos on YouTube that can show you how. If you don't understand a business concept, or how to integrate a specific app, how to use a contact database, or how to tweet, then it is all there, free of charge. You can learn how to navigate the changing social media programs easily and effectively with no investment but your time and interest.

Social media and communications platforms like Vimeo, YouTube, Kahn Academy, Curriki, and Udemy are excellent learning platforms—most of which are completely free. When you feel stumped by a process or how to implement a new device or program, search those information dispensing tools for possible video solutions and trainings. You may not be alone in your concern or inquiry. Your confidence will grow as you seek out answers and solutions that grow your business as opposed to deciding it's too hard to learn or you're not smart enough. Realize, again, that the most important things are to connect with other people and nurture relationships. Find mediums that nurture you, as well, and technologies that grow you personally.

Knowing how to implement each platform into your work goals and understanding how to use the data they each provide you are critical. These are not difficult things to learn. Most companies today know the value of making things user-friendly. They build these technologies so anyone can use them.

To me, the key is the implementation. Some time ago, I wanted to learn how to create a photobook online, as I love taking photos. But then, I had to decide what to do with my vast digital library (over 20,000 images). It took me a while to learn the methods of creating a great photobook; but once I did, I used it to share with others and deepen relationships.

Two quick examples. First, a year or so ago, my wife and I were invited to represent the State of Utah on our Governor's Trade Mission to the nation of Israel. It was an outstanding week. I took my camera and documented many of our meetings and conferences. *The next step is the one most people won't take.* I memorialized our trip there by creating a photobook of the Trade Mission and made copies for five different folks who accompanied us there. No one asked me to do this. I just thought it would be a nice gesture to my fellow business colleagues. It included pictures of us with Benjamin Netanyahu, interactions with some of the top venture capital funds in Israel, and several trips to the top universities in Israel, as well as some sacred sites we visited together.

Second, several months later, I found myself at a concert memorializing the life of Bob Engemann, one of the original members of the Letterman, a spectacularly successful singing group from the 50's and 60's. Bobby is the uncle of our good friend Shawn King, wife of Larry King. The performers that night included an amazing array of talent. I happened to sit in the front row with my wife, and we captured hundreds of great photos. I created a subset of 50 of them and built them into a photobook that was then given to nine members of the King and Engemann families. They were so appreciative of this extra-mile effort that it has cemented our relationship forever.

I tell you these things not to brag about our trips or impress you with the people that we know, but rather to tell you that *you can and should do it too.* The deepening of relationships that has occurred from sharing a few photos is amazing and will continue to bless our lives for years to come.

You will find that these technologies, once learned, become assets to you in other areas of relationships, such as staying in touch with family members who live far away, creating digital photo albums to share, growing a non-profit globally, tutoring a grandchild long-distance, finding your ancestors or family history, and managing a high school reunion. Your capacity to nurture relationships through understanding technology can do more than just drive you to the top of your profession and increase your business wealth. It can, and should, increase the depth and purpose of your life and inspire others to do the same.

Take a class. Second, as technology evolves, you may want to understand certain programs or processes in more depth. Through local business groups, libraries, or local education sources, you can find classes on Word Press, Facebook, and social media that can inexpensively teach you the ins and outs of systems to reach more people. One benefit to taking classes is meeting more people! Learn at least one new technique, program, or strategy each quarter—this means four new processes a year. This plan gives you three months of learning and application before you venture out and learn another. If you find one process isn't a good fit for you, then move on to learning another so the tools in your tool belt are multiplied each year, making next year far more productive than this year, and so on. Your database can be growing as you learn and implement.

Hire an assistant. Third, and this would be my last option, you can hire someone to manage your systems for you. Under your direction, this person can categorize your systems in ways that help you locate, log, manage, and track your interactions so that you can easily find your contacts in the context you desire. This may be a part-time or full-time administrator, a secretary, or an office manager. A term that is used frequently in today's marketplace is "VA" or "virtual assistant." Working remotely, a VA can manage your database effectively and effortlessly, giving you more time to connect personally. My encouragement is to learn the programs and connect with people personally rather than outsource this process. While it takes time to learn new tools, the best person to project you and your personality is you.

Technostress is common, and all of us suffer from it on some level. But overcoming it is essential for nurturing relationships through technology. By going at your own speed, sharing meaningful information, and becoming educated, you can make your technological prowess an asset rather than a liability when developing your social capital. Leaders are those who know how to harness the technologies of today.

Develop Social Capital

No matter what platform or medium you employ, the goal is to create depth in relationships. This is your "social capital." Today, some of the best vehicles to grow depth in your business relationships are Facebook, Instagram, LinkedIn, Twitter, and Google+. Innovative technologies can boost your efficiency by connecting faster and with a broader range of people. You can grow your relationships on these platforms, specifically, by inspiring with quotes, encouraging personal communication, reaching out, and following through.

Inspire with quotes. One of the ways that I like to employ today's social media tools is to encourage others with uplifting quotes. As mentioned earlier, almost daily I post thoughts and quotes from great thinkers and leaders. In this way, I can reach my contacts, perhaps give them mental fuel for their day's challenges, and, in doing so, share part of myself with them. This is not for any profit or gain other than to grow and nurture the connections we have between us. Doing this does take time. I look for quotes to share that I feel have value and merit. I choose quotes without agenda or force and make sure they will not offend or intimidate. As simple a task as this is, the reward has been significant. Those in my contact list that I know less well have reason to respond, ask questions, make comments, and move to greater depth in our relationship.

Just the other day, I was deeply touched by a message from a Facebook friend whom I had not seen in three years. On a typical morning, I had found a cool quote and shared it on Facebook. This one was from Deepak Chopra and read as follows: "All great changes are preceded by chaos."

After reading the quote, my friend Sumeet wrote the following:

> Hi David. Love your inspirational thoughts. I found this one very comforting. My life at the moment is total chaos. I lost my mother to cancer about 20 months ago and then lost my father unexpectedly 3 months ago. I have had to stop my work at Fusion-io so that I can be in Delhi to sort out my father's affairs. My family is still in California. It's tough, but I always find comfort in the things you share.

I don't know about you, but I cried when I read his note. Once again, lives were touched and a relationship was deepened.

Encourage personal communication. Efforts to create top-of-mind awareness are most effective when used in conjunction with in-person connections. My email and Facebook communications often lead to meeting in person. With a visit, a lunch meeting, or even a phone call, the relationship then moves to a deeper level. There is no better reinforcement or self-marketing strategy that trumps a live interaction where genuine rapport can be created and felt. Using technology to initiate a one-on-one meeting, as well as to follow up and stay connected, creates a powerful dynamic. How can you translate this into your business routine? Who can you invite to lunch? Who can you stop by and visit?

Earlier this year, my wife was looking to expand the footprint for her 3D online virtual world technology. In particular, she was looking to partner with an online university. On this very same topic, I reconnected after years with my old friend Graham Doxey, CEO of KNOD, a Global Learning University. We exchanged some LinkedIn messages. The result was another great in-person meeting and the potential to embed Linda's 3D classrooms into the Global Learning University. Moral of the story: Sometimes you need to first meet virtually and follow with an in-person meeting to cement the relationship.

If this sounds intimidating, then there may be opportunities to work or volunteer in ways that connect you with others. Networking via a shared cause can create connections and bonds that are fulfilling and beneficial. Find something you are passionate about so you can relax and enjoy yourself. This will enable you to communicate clearly and effectively, presenting yourself in a transparent, authentic manner.

Reach out. Grow your existing networks, which are the groups of people that you associate with naturally. Church group, sports teams, and neighbors are obvious examples. After becoming part of a group, find common points of interest with people. People are fascinating. Find out what makes them tick, and you will become a natural networker. Show genuine interest and support. Collect contact information as a natural form of meeting people, and use it to maintain communication. Share articles, recipes, carpooling, and serve their needs and interests as you genuinely can. Showing a genuine interest in people will enable you to naturally and organically grow your network.

Recently, following a lecture I delivered at a college, one of the students wrote to me and asked:

Date: 11/8/13

Hi David,

I had a question as a result of your lecture at BYU this morning about networking. I've always felt like I don't network as much as I should because I often find myself feeling not really interested in finding out about the other person when I have opportunities to meet people and network with them. I can and sometimes do push that aside and get to know them anyway, but I was wondering if you have any suggestions for increasing my interest in other people so I can take advantage of more networking opportunities. I appreciate any help you can give. Thank you for your time.

Brian M.

My response was as follows:

Brian, Dale Carnegie once said:

"You can make more friends in two months by becoming interested in other people than you can in two years by trying to get other people interested in you."

But what I hear on your end is a lack of motivation to get interested. To me, the missing piece to this dilemma is *finding common points of interest.*

You are quite right—it is difficult to always show real interest. Let's say you are talking to someone, and you find yourself being disinterested. How do you turn your interest level around and make the interchange more fascinating for both of you?

The answer is to find a topic that interests both parties. Note: You can only do this by asking a lot of questions.

- Tell me about your hometown.
- What are you passionate about in life?
- What is the toughest problem you face at work?
- What do you like to do in your spare time?
- Who is your personal idol?
- What is your favorite movie of all time?
- Tell me about your favorite job.

Once you hit upon a topic of mutual interest, the conversation will flow naturally. Over time, as you explore areas of commonality, trust begins to form. And when trust ensues, your willingness to engage fully and be of assistance to the other person increases. As mentioned elsewhere in this book, when trust exists, everything accelerates in a positive manner with your new friend.

Follow through. This is one of the most important elements of growing a network with (or without) technology. If you promise to do something for someone, then *do it.* If you arrange a meeting, then go. Be real. Then stay in touch with the use of technology, and continue to follow up. Use the steps I share later in this book on organizing your contacts. This will make following up and staying connected even easier.

Over time, your network and depth of connections will grow exponentially. The quality and quantity of that growth may not be easily seen in its early stages, but inspiring others with quotes and other meaningful messages, focusing on personal connections, reaching out, and following through can help you win and lead in business. Start building your network and growing your social capital early so that it can be a valuable, growing asset throughout your career.

Conclusion

Some use the term "networking" to describe the activity of amassing large numbers of contacts. This psychology is contrary to what I believe is a timeless truth. Now, even with over 20,000 contacts in my network, I understand that to be effective in business I must build and nurture *deep* relationships. The total number of connections is not nearly as important as the depth of the connections. However, make no mistake: quantity can translate into quality if one is adept. The goal can never be about growing the number without true connection. The goal is to connect in a way, and to a depth, with each of those people that I am able to name, locate, organize, and manage individuals that have certain skills in specific areas. I want to know what my Facebook friends and LinkedIn contacts need so I can serve them and share resources. That is where the power lies. That is what will drive you to the top of your game.

I absolutely loved this email received via LinkedIn from a young lady that attended one of my recent lectures. To me, it captures the most valuable part of networking.

Hi Mr. Bradford,

I actually went back and looked at my notes from your lecture, and what impressed me the most was how my misconception of networking was dispelled. I used to think that networking meant manipulating people you know to get something you wanted, but during your talk I really came to see that it is more about building relationships with people that you respect and with whom you want to work. You don't have to (and probably shouldn't) network with people that you don't like or who you don't respect, so it's really about making fun connections—people you can help and who can help you. That's what I enjoyed the most about your presentation. As far as your book title is concerned, I would say you should call it, "The Networking Lifestyle." Thanks so much again!

Sincerely,
Ashley M.

What words of encouragement can you say to others that will enhance their abilities to succeed in life? That sort of support can deepen your relationships and form personal connections that will benefit everyone down the road!

CHAPTER 2 GAME PLAN

1. A tectonic change in networking has been enabled by online social media. But remember, the most important thing is to build deep relationships. Social media is only a means to an end.

2. Remember, don't force anything when you are trying to network—in fact, don't try to "network." Just work on developing solid and real relationships.

3. Business is all about connecting. The more you connect, the more deeply you connect; and the more credibly you connect, the more success you will have.

4. People wonder at my capacity to get so many things done seemingly simultaneously. Let me tell you my dirty little secret: I don't have just one or two friends helping me solve my business issues, I have thousands of them via social media.

5. Start building your network early so that it can be a valuable, growing asset throughout your career.

6. Today there are over 2.5 billion users of the web, versus 16 million in 1995. Yet, how many of those users know the value of the time spent online in Facebook, Instagram, Twitter or LinkedIn? And how many know the importance of their integrity and personal brand while using it?

PRINCIPLE 1: START UP

When Linda and I were first married over 40 years ago, we visited a little shop in Santa Monica, California, that displayed some beautiful prose: "To love is to give with no thought of getting." Linda is a professional calligrapher, among other things, and created a beautiful plaque displaying the aphorism that hangs on our library wall to this day.

As simple as it sounds, this maxim embodies the first principle of effective networking. Start up your game by giving with no thought of getting. Love truly is the essential foundation upon which relationships are built. When you approach others—and they know you care for them and are really genuinely interested in helping them—you are following the law of reciprocity and taking the necessary first steps to building a lasting, rewarding network from which you will benefit both personally and monetarily. These budding relationships are then nurtured with time, emotional investment, and service, and bloom into lasting friendships of mutual support—the ultimate goal of networking.

Thus, as you think about starting up and stepping up your game, it all should begin with thinking first of others. I always emphasize, in the speeches I give, the importance of walking into a business networking event with the mindset of uncovering what the other people at the event are there looking for and how I might assist them. Recently, I gave an executive lecture to several large classes at a prominent college business school. I was gratified by some of the comments I received back that reinforced the importance of giving without a thought of getting in launching your network.

One student by the name of Nate wrote to me via LinkedIn following the lecture and said:

> In regards to your lecture: I always thought networking seemed very self-centered. It felt like using people for my own ends. What you taught, however, was the important piece I was missing: networking should be about the other person. I need to ask myself, "What can I do for them?" and by this approach networking becomes much more beneficial and desirable to both parties.
>
> Nate M.

Another student by the name of Eric wrote to me and added these insights:

> The main thing that I got out of your message is to help others. I had never really looked at business as a service opportunity, but I realized that I was missing the point. Starting networking relationships with the principle of giving with no thought of getting is so obvious, but I didn't get it. In the past, I was always trying to strike a deal, especially because I'm at a point in my life where I am looking for help all the time. I didn't think that I have much to offer, but I now realize that it's the complete

opposite. I can help others and will feel good because of it. Perhaps it will help me in the long run. So, giving without the thought of getting is the point that stuck out to me the most.

Eric P.

The Law of Reciprocity

The law of reciprocity dictates that when we help others, help will return to us down the road in some form. In business and personal relationships, I can confirm the truth of the adage, "Relationships are investments—the more you put in, the more you get back." But here's the irony of the situation: for the law of reciprocity to work, you have to be motivated to give because you desire to serve, not because you have an expectation for reward.

When you invest in others without controlling the outcome or imposing your interests, people feel a great sense of loyalty. It has been shown that great leaders have a gift of showing compassion for others, and it helps drive their success. By supporting *their* goals and celebrating *their* victories, others will automatically be drawn to do the same for you. As Ralph Waldo Emerson states, "It is one of the most beautiful compensations of life that no man can sincerely try to help another without helping himself." When you give your time, emotional capital, and resources, the law of reciprocity will send that goodwill right back to you and help you network your way to the top.

Give Your Time

Someone once said that if you really want to give someone a gift, try giving them your time and attention. Giving people your time is essential to building strong relationships. In 2011, I was assisting Dave Checketts, former President of Madison Square Garden and the New York Knicks, in raising a significant venture fund to invest in professional sports franchises around the globe.

As usual, my life was filled with a number of fun and interesting activities, including building a couple of successful business enterprises.

During this time, I was contacted by an out-of-work sales representative. This rep (we'll call him "John") was an individual that I had met back in 1994 when I was a Senior Vice President of Novell. We had acquired the Word Perfect Corporation, for whom he worked. Years later, John and I had connected on LinkedIn and had stayed in touch.

John called me on the phone and began our conversation by saying, "Dave, I have been out of work for nearly a year. I love to sell and feel like I have some good expertise in selling technology. I know you are active in tech circles. Can you go to lunch with me and allow me to pick your brain on potential job opportunities?"

My initial reaction was, "How do I get out of this? I am just too busy to do another lunch." But then my thoughts went back to my father who was a sales representative for many years. I knew the stress and anxiety John must have been feeling. I was sure he had a family and that he was undoubtedly the principal breadwinner. After a long pause, I responded. "Sure. When and where do you want to do lunch?"

A couple of days passed, and we found ourselves in a 90-minute lunch. I gave my newly reconnected friend referrals to four tech CEOs in Utah that were hiring. At the close of our lunch, and to his credit, this man said, "David, I can't thank you enough for these referrals. I will be following up with them. What can I do for you?"

"That's all right. I am good. Just busy," I responded.

"No Dave," John insisted. "Honestly, what are you working on? Maybe I can provide a helping hand in some way."

"Well, I am helping Dave Checketts raise a $250 million investment fund for the sports world."

John thought for a moment and then said, "Hmm. I actually know someone who might have an interest!"

He then proceeded to take action. He reached out to a friend of his named Jim whom he met some years earlier in the Middle East. Turns out John's buddy was the chief financial advisor to a wealthy Saudi prince. That very afternoon John reached out to Jim. Upon further investigation, John learned that the Prince was currently staying in his home in Beverly Hills. John then introduced me to this prince. Since the prince was in Beverly Hills on Pacific Time, he agreed that afternoon to meet with me the very next day. I jumped on a plane to Los Angeles that night. The next morning at 11 a.m., the prince greeted me warmly, and we had a great two-hour meeting with some of his financial advisors. In the end, the prince expressed strong interest in committing potentially millions to invest in the fund. John also secured a sales position with one of the referrals I gave him. Who would have ever thought that an out-of-work sales rep would provide me with a very substantial multimillion-dollar connection?

Here is the takeaway: Take the time to help people. You never ever know who may be the one that introduces you to a life-changing opportunity or experience. When we respond to the needs of others with no thought of what we might get out of it, the universe conspires to facilitate powerful and wonderfully reciprocal business and personal relationships.

Giving your time is not only important in the moment, as in the lunch with John, but also in the long term. Many of my important relationships have developed over time, often over decades. People feel they can call on me for a favor and vice versa.

Give Your Emotional Capital

We are all human beings with a universal desire to feel wanted, valued, and appreciated. Each one of us hungers for connection. Whether you are a celebrity or the average Joe on the street, personal interaction—especially at a deep level—is significant. In many instances, it is the employee inside of a large corporation that feels underappreciated and unrecognized. This is where a great leader can stand up, reach out, and give emotional support.

A study was done a few years ago of business leaders. It found that there is a strong link between worker productivity and what has been identified as "compassionate leadership" in organizations. Christina Boedker, a lecturer in accounting at the Australian School of Business, led a major research study that studied the links between leadership and performance. She observed that the single greatest influence on profitability and productivity within a firm is the ability of leaders to spend more time and effort developing and recognizing their people, welcoming feedback, including criticism, and fostering cooperation among staff.

Boedker observed: "Out of all of the various elements in a business, the ability of a leader to be compassionate, that is, "to understand people's motivators, hopes, and difficulties, and to create the right support mechanism to allow people to be as good as they can be," has the greatest correlation with profitability and productivity. "It's about valuing people and being receptive and responsive to criticism."

A great example of a compassionate leader is HireVue's CEO, Mark Newman. Though young in years, he possesses a mature spirit, and it shows in his relationships with his employees whom he calls his "team members." I recently shared an email with our board of directors from one of the members of the HireVue team. She wrote: "This is the best place I have ever had the opportunity to work. Between everyone's dedication to success, spreading the credit for all of the hard work, creating a culture that allows risks, doesn't kick you out the door for failures, putting our military heroes in the front of everyone's mind so that they can get back to work at the end of their service, and for making everyone that works here feel valued and appreciated every day. It just doesn't get any better than this. So happy to be on the team!" This is due primarily to the culture built by Mr. Newman. He loves his team members and it shows in his style and leadership.

As seen above, people love it when you show up for them physically and emotionally—to have their back, so to speak. When you practice this principle of giving first without thinking about what you may receive, then you truly have Upped Your Game.

Speaking of games, in 1994, Steve Young, then quarterback of the San Francisco 49ers, casually invited our family to the Super Bowl Championship game that was being played against the San Diego Chargers. We adjusted our schedules to participate, and we were not disappointed. It was a phenomenal opportunity and a one-of-a-kind event in which Steve broke the all-time NFL record for most touchdown passes in a Super Bowl and was named Most Valuable Player for Super Bowl XXIX. After the game, Steve was hospitalized due to dehydration, and we went to the hospital to see him. Steve raised his IV-infused arms as we entered the room and said: "You showed up! You came! Can you believe I threw six touchdown passes? I never threw six touchdown passes in any of my pee-wee football games! Thank you, thank you for coming."

Being there in the hospital that day, at that pivotal moment in Steve's life, cemented our relationship. When we show up for other people and emotionally invest in them—their illnesses, injuries, celebrations, and accomplishments—we develop common experiences that begin lasting friendships. Those deep relationships are mutually supportive and become reciprocal as others also show up for us in our lives at times we are in need.

My relationship with Steve Young continued to develop over time. In the late 90's, we went down to Arizona together, where Steve went on his first date with his future wife, Barb. Later in

1999, we all spent a week together in Israel. That incredibly spiritual and emotional trip strengthened the ties we shared. Through many years and through many of life's experiences, Steve and I have been close friends. This has extended to our wives and our children. In fact, Steve and Barb's oldest son, Braden, received his baby blessing in our home.

In my efforts to grow my companies over the years, Steve has served as an advisor to many of them. A law school graduate and member of many boards of directors, Steve had a successful post-football career as a managing partner of Huntsman-Gay Equity Partners. When a given company needed introductions to specific accounts, Steve came through. He washed dishes with the young founder and eventual CEO of HireVue. He kindly signed footballs for key customers, prospective employees, and strategic alliances. He came through in a big way with a key Fusion-io account. And he helped introduce us into some of the accounts where we had issues breaking through.

At one extremely important meeting with the Vice Chairman of the board of Samsung, who was a big 49ers fan, we presented a football signed by the two Steves: Steve Young and Steve Wozniak. Both, at the time, were Fusion-io advisory board members. The gratitude of this normally reserved and dignified senior Samsung executive was palpable.

Steve's attitude was giving with no thought of getting. He thought of my needs first despite an incredibly busy business schedule with commitments to ESPN and his world of private equity. Steve's dedication and help came not only from his personal character, but also from our mutual support and reciprocal friendship. Our relationship is strong because we have both invested emotional capital in it, and that capital has yielded compound interest over time.

Give Your Resources

Of all the powerful relationships in my life and career, none has equaled the significance of my marriage partnership with my wife, Linda. As the CEO of a virtual online educational program, Linda is a professional in her own right. But that is where our similarities in management style end. She is a structured, measured person, while I tend to shoot from the hip. She will plan out the details of a family vacation six months in advance, while I would want to wait until two weeks beforehand to let the kids know where we are going. This difference could have created conflict between us, but instead Linda has been my greatest teacher. Her strengths have taught me to be a better husband, father, and businessperson.

Let me tell you of an experience Linda and I shared a number of years ago when someone went out of their way to bless our lives with a great and much-needed gift of resources. But first some background . . .

I first met Linda in the fall of 1972 when I was attending BYU. We were both in the same English class, and I was mesmerized by her hair. We were both straight-A students, but I tended to be the jokester in class, while Linda was more serious.

Our first date was in December of 1972. We went sledding with my church group. Everything seemed to be going very well until one of the girls in the group broke her back. The ambulance took her to the hospital, and we followed behind. I watched Linda as she responded to the girl's trauma. I saw the way she managed a crisis situation under stress and how she cared for this girl who was hurting. I was impressed.

Later that night, we went to Long John Silver's in Provo and then to a basketball game at the school. The next day, we went to a church fireside together. After that, I only dated Linda.

Shortly after Valentine's Day, I knelt in the snow and proposed to her in her backyard. We were married in August 1973. Our partnership has been the foundation of our family and, ultimately, the foundation of the most important board upon which I sit. As we talk about nurturing relationships, this is where our skills make the most impact. How do our listening skills and giving skills really play out in our day-to-day relationships? Are we finding common ground in our family relationships? Are we creating environments of mutual support and encouragement in our primary relationships? Those who know you best can give you the best advice, the best feedback, and the best support. Nurture those relationships, and let them be a resource to you, as well. These are the relationships that require you to give without getting, invest of yourself, and serve without agenda or control.

As we began our lives as a couple, money was very tight, and the stress was difficult. One night, we heard a knock at the door of our tiny home in Canyon Country, California. Following the knock, a car sped off into the night. As I looked out the window, I could see a sack in front of the door. At the time, I was practicing law, and there were some weird clients. I was worried it might be a bomb or some sort of explosive device. On my guard, based on what I'd seen in my schooling, I told Linda, "Let's just leave it there and go to bed." About an hour later the phone rang. An ominous voice, said, "Look out your front door step."

I looked out again and saw the sack. I said to Linda, "Let's go back and wait until morning. Then we'll figure this out." About 2:00 in the morning the phone rang again. The voice again said emphatically, "Look out your front door!" The strained voice was so insistent and so demanding, we were scared. So, we called the cops. Within half an hour, we saw the red and white lights flashing down the street. This time, a police officer knocked at the door.

"Mr. Bradford," he said, "I think you can come out now." We opened the door and saw not one sack of groceries but two. And around the corner, in front of our garage, there were four more sacks of groceries. The mystery voice had left us six bags of groceries with fresh meat and vegetables and dairy. The voice wanted to make sure we put it into the refrigerator because it was perishable. We were speechless.

For 35 years, we were clueless as to who had performed this magnificent kindness. Then, in the spring of 2013, Linda and I found ourselves in the Salt Lake airport preparing for a flight to Southern California. Virtually, out of nowhere, an old friend named Greg Crow came up to me and gave me a big bear hug. The last time we had seen Greg was over 30 years earlier when we were living in Southern California. Greg had gone on to a great career as a Sheriff with the city of Los Angeles. As we reminisced while we waited for our plane, Greg said,"Hey, David and Linda, remember when I used to work at the 7/11 in Canyon Country?" We both nodded, "Yes."

Greg continued, "Well, do you remember David Fretz and Ron Riddle?" We said, "Sure. They were part of our LDS Church congregation."

Greg went on: "Let me share with you something I still remember to this day. One night, David and Ron came into my 7/11 store. They said that the Bradfords needed help. They were determined to find a way to bring you some food. So they proceeded to buy out the store of milk, bread, and fresh meat to deliver to your home that night."

After Greg finished relaying this memory, Linda and I were stunned. The mystery of who blessed our lives with their resources so many years earlier had been solved. Imagine the surprise and emotions that flooded us when we finally realized who had been so kind to us at this critical juncture of our lives.

But I am happy to report that, over the years, we have paid that kindness forward. We were so touched by the kindness that had been shown to us that year when we were struggling financially that we made a personal vow to reciprocate. Every Christmas for the last 34 years, we have found a family in need, and late on every Christmas Eve, we ding dong ditch while delivering groceries, toys, and other goodies to one of these families. Thirty-four Christmas Eves and families have been blessed because David Fretz and Ron Riddle took the time to care for us. David and Ron truly Upped Their Game that night, and the blessing has carried through to others for almost 35 years.

Just like the mystery voice did for us, Linda and I, as a team, try to find opportunities to give. That makes our partnership stronger. Supporting other people's ventures and dreams makes us stronger as individuals, as well. Not because we get something from it, but because of who we become in the process of giving and serving. Nurturing relationships comes from a desire to help people, not from a desire to get something from people. Others sense that. When your caring and support are genuine, they remember your acts of kindness and how you impacted them. It can impact them for years, even decades.

How do you nurture the people around you? How do you get onboard with their goals and aspirations? How can you help them get to the resources that would put them one step closer to realizing a benchmark in their career or with their company? What can you do to celebrate their victories with them? Through Facebook, especially, you can keep current on what people are participating in, what they are pursuing, and what they are doing with their families and their businesses. Through LinkedIn you can follow people's career paths, their educational pursuits, and their transitions in employment. I make it a regular habit, when I see someone has been promoted or changed jobs, to send them a personal note of congratulations.

Following people and staying in touch are essential principles that I will touch on later in the book, but here I want to focus on giving without getting. Your connections with people need to take place at the turning points in their lives, not only when there is a point of sale. Invest in their successes even if it is through simple means. Often the least extravagant methods prove to be the most memorable.

Recently, my sister and brother-in-law received a letter that included a call from their church to dedicate the next 18 months of their life to serve in a foreign country. The day came when they were going to open the letter and discover to which nation they would be assigned to serve. My day was filled with meetings and responsibilities, but I did not want to miss the moment they opened the letter to find out the location of their mission. Fighting traffic to arrive before the envelope was opened, I pulled out my camera and began clicking away. It was an exciting time for all of us in the room. I was so proud of my sister and brother-in-law and wanted to capture the feeling for them somehow. Later that night, I sat at the computer and put together a slideshow with the pictures of their experience.

Conclusion

It was not a hard thing for me to do a slide show for them. It was simple, really. Just as I said in the introduction of this book, my advice is simple. Because it is so simple, you may think it rather insignificant or antiquated. You may not act on the principles I've been sharing. However, it is the simplicity of nurturing relationships that has helped me build a successful career. As a boy who came from shoveling coal into my parents' heater because we could not afford a normal furnace, I have had incredible opportunities to rub shoulders with the best and greatest minds, athletes, performers, and thinkers of this world—and I believe it has been because of a very simple relationship principle: Start up by giving with no thought of getting.

I share this with you again to help you see that relationships develop with time, mutual support, emotional investment, and service. The law of reciprocity will manifest in ways that will benefit you years down the road and in ways that you could never imagine. To have many satisfying relationships of this nature is the ultimate goal of networking.

Are you really willing to start up your game and give with no thought of getting?

CHAPTER 3 GAME PLAN

1. Networking is truly more about giving than getting. When making a new contact, your first thought should be: "How can I help this new acquaintance?"

2. Offer to write a blog post for someone or offer to post an event or project to your social media platforms.

3. Let people know you are following them and care about what they are doing. Tag people in social media. Let them know you are thinking about them. It makes them feel valued and appreciated.

4. Remember that there is a law of reciprocity in the universe. Give as much or more than you receive; otherwise, your network will dry up.

5. Go serve somewhere—a soup kitchen, the Red Cross, or your church. Your efforts to serve others will be noticed and will engender feelings of trust.

6. Do a special "thank you" for those that really help you out —give them a new golf club, a day at the spa, or tickets to a movie or play.

PRINCIPLE 2: SHOW UP

I am fond of the classic mantra that 90 percent of success in life is achieved just by showing up. To impact people's lives personally, professionally, or financially, you must create a presence. They must see you, experience you, and be engaged by you. This requires you to show up in memorable and effective ways in their lives. This principle demands that you take action based on the premise that people have intrinsic value and that you should be present for them. When you take this action, the stars align and open up possibilities that did not exist prior to your involvement. Often it is as easy as just being in the room, shaking hands with an individual, or being a bystander in a particular conversation. In short, when you show up, things happen. This principle is exemplified by a series of events that turned into what I refer to as "a game-changing connection." As you shall see, when we show up to serve, create top-of-mind awareness, inspire mutual growth, build relationships, and exchange services, we step up our games, and our billion-dollar network builds itself organically and effortlessly.

The Game Changer

Most of us are familiar with the importance of showing up at meetings, conferences, weddings, church, soccer games, and the like. So much good can come from the interactions we have at those events. But sometimes it takes vision and patience to see how these key connections come together.

This became ever more apparent in July of 2008 when I "showed up" at a conference in Sun Valley, Idaho, the result of which was an incredibly fortuitous meeting with Steve Wozniak, the inventor of the Apple computer. That meeting was the beginning of a friendship and business relationship that has now spanned the course of five years, resulting in Steve joining our team at Fusion-io as Chief Scientist. It is an example of how being in the right place at the right time can align a trajectory of positive events that would otherwise never happen. But it is also an example of how seemingly minor meetings and interactions can make a massive difference in your business life.

The story of how I attracted the inventor of the Apple computer to Fusion-io begins with my daughter Angela. Angela lives in Utah close to our home in Provo. At the time, she was about to give birth to her fourth child, Moti. Her obstetrician was Dr. Tom Judd. He was a baby doctor with a grundle of children of his own—nine of them, in fact.

After watching Tom flawlessly deliver this precious grandchild of mine, he asked me to eat breakfast with him. As I recall, it was eggs and hash browns. As we chatted, Tom mentioned his son-in-law, Brian LeBrecht. Brian had married one of Tom's daughters. He explained that Brian was busy establishing his new law practice and needed some help generating clients. I remembered my days in Southern California and frantically trying to find accounts. That had been a very challenging time for me, as I had no connections in that area. I felt sympathetic to Brian's plight and clearly understood how intimidating the process could be. Tom asked if I could meet with his son-in-law and share any advice I might have to help build his client base.

I thought of my busy schedule. I thought of my other responsibilities. But I reluctantly agreed to help because of my respect and friendship with Tom—and because I believe in the principle of showing up for people. Often it is not convenient or easy. It requires adjusting, scheduling, maneuvering, and committing. It requires taking meetings when requested. It requires giving help when needed. It requires listening and advising. But it can bless the life of another in important ways and will likely be of benefit to you in the long run. In this particular case, I could never have imagined how the outcome of our conversation over eggs and hash browns would impact me directly down the road.

Several months after my breakfast with Dr. Tom, I showed up at the scheduled date and met with Brian. I was curious about his needs and how I could help him. One suggestion I made was to get involved in some community organizations that would increase his visibility and presence in the legal community. I explained to him the value of networking principles, especially the value of showing up to community events that would allow himself, his skills, his personality, and his talents to be seen, utilized, and appreciated.

Six months passed. Brian followed my advice and called to give me an update on his progress. "Mr. Bradford, I took your advice. I joined the volunteer side at the Utah Bar Association, and I am now on the speaker's bureau for the group. I'd like to invite you to speak at our upcoming annual lawyer's convention in Sun Valley, Idaho." I was flattered but, checking Google Maps and calculating the distance, I was hesitant. It was at least a five-hour drive from my home in Provo, Utah. After giving it some thought, I accepted the invitation to speak.

Little did I know that the stars were aligning in my favor with one very exciting introduction awaiting me. As I packed up my car to make the drive, I figured it would be good for me to take a break from my hectic routine. Throwing my fishing pole and golf clubs in the back, I happily drove the 300 miles to beautiful Sun Valley to speak at the convention.

The speech went well. Afterwards, as I was leaving the venue to head back to Utah, a young lawyer stopped me. He was very complimentary of my presentation and wanted to thank me for my remarks. I was anxious to leave, as I pictured myself playing golf at one of Sun Valley's best golfing venues on my way back home. This young lawyer, however, was highly animated and passionate about our conversation. As he talked, I glanced down and saw a piece of paper that had Steve Wozniak's name on it. Now, a bit distracted and intrigued at seeing this impressive name, I picked up the paper and noted to my astonishment that the man who co-founded Apple Computer would be the luncheon keynote speaker!

I had a choice to make: Stay or go. Often in our lives, both professionally and personally, we are faced with this choice. I had planned to play golf in Sun Valley. Now, with this new information, I was presented with a difficult decision. I had the opportunity to hear Steve Wozniak, but I love golf and really wanted to play. One of my favorite quotes from a respected religious leader, M. Russell Ballard, says this: "Small events and choices determine the direction of our lives just as small helms determine the direction of great ships." My choice that day seemed a small one. The outcome, however, was priceless. Ask yourself this: "What decision will I make today about establishing a connection or showing up that could change the course of my life?"

I turned around and walked into the convention center—a rounded room that seated more than 500 people. I remember thinking to myself: "If I am going to be here, I am going to be right up front and as close as possible to this industry giant!" I made my way to the front row and sat down next to a young woman pounding away on her Apple computer next to me. She looked up, and we exchanged "hellos" and began talking. To my surprise, the woman next to me, Julie Roebuck, was Mr. Wozniak's assistant!

Julie and I spoke for a few minutes about our industries and roles. When I described my work and that I had been connected to the computer industry for over 25 years, she excitedly said, "Oh, you will have to meet Steve! He doesn't usually speak in front of lawyers, and he will be happy to know there is another computer guy in the room!" Putting Steve and me in the same category of "computer guys" seemed laughable, but I was thrilled at the thought of having an introduction to such a revolutionary individual.

Steve Wozniak transformed the way we engage with technology. He is the quintessential icon. From his name to his persona to his inventions, "Woz" is clearly someone that future generations will regard as having had an enormous impact on the twentieth and twenty-first centuries of technology. In 1970, Steve Wozniak and Steve Jobs became friends. From there, these two formed the company known around the world as "Apple Computer." Working in the bedroom and later the garage of Steve Job's home, Wozniak assembled the first prototypes of what would later become the "Apple 1." Many compared it to a work of art. The hardware and the software operating system for this first Apple computer all came from the mind, talent, skill, and hard work of one man: Steve Wozniak.

After he finished speaking that day, Steve approached Julie, his assistant. She immediately introduced us. I was thrilled to meet Steve and shared with him my quick background, including my fourteen-plus years at Novell. He mentioned that he knew some of the technical team there. Asking me what I did presently, I explained my current affiliation with a company by the name of Fusion-io and the groundbreaking work we were doing with SSDs (Solid State Disks). He, too, was excited about the potential of SSDs and asked me to send him some materials on Fusion-io.

Given Steve's initial interest, I wanted to get back to him right away. (Note: to "follow up" quickly and personally is another one of the six key principles.)

Arriving back in Utah late that night, I shot Steve an email.

July 18, 2008

Steve, you added a lot today and made the Utah Bar meetings worth attending. My career in the law included 15 years as General Counsel of Novell, but these days I am mostly a web guy. I guess you would categorize me as a social entrepreneur, having started three web-based companies, including www.FundingUniverse.com and www.LinkingUniverse.com.

On a separate note, I have been talking to our mutual friend, Shawn Nunley, recently about a company by the name of Fusion-io. The Fusion-io Drive is a high-density, extremely fast memory extension or drive replacement based on flash memory technology. Fusion-io also just inked a major deal with Hewlett-Packard.

I am an advisor to the company and thought you might be interested at some level. Please check them out and give me your thoughts. http://fusionio.com/

David

I kept my fingers crossed for a response. It did not take long. Great leaders, including Woz, follow up. He responded within 24 hours and said that he would be "delighted" to join our advisory board.

This, of course, was an exciting response. To have a man the stature of Steve Wozniak join our advisory board and tacitly endorse our technology could be a game changer. I then set up a meeting between Woz and David Flynn and Rick While, who were the co-founders of Fusion-io. As I suspected, the techies hit it off wonderfully. Shortly thereafter, I became CEO of Fusion-io, and Mr. Wozniak became my Chief Scientist. According to Steve, this was his first employee "paycheck" since Apple.

During this time, Steve was competing in "Dancing with the Stars" and was in Southern California frequently. I made a concerted effort to stay in touch with Steve, organizing his first sales call on behalf of Fusion with MySpace.com. The result was the biggest order for Fusion-io technology received up to that point.

I believe it is instructive to walk through the things that had to transpire in order to make all of this happen. As I list the steps that took place through the course of this story, it may be helpful for you as my reader to recognize that all of these action items are simple and doable for you in your realm of influence, as well. The principles outlined in this book support the small steps needed for fruition and positive outcomes.

1. I showed up at the birth of my grandchild and had breakfast with the obstetrician.
2. The obstetrician asked me to meet his son-in-law.
3. I met with the son-in-law, Brian.
4. Brian followed my advice, became involved in community organizations, and was appointed chairman of the speaker's bureau for the Utah Bar Association.
5. Brian asked me to speak at the event in Sun Valley.
6. I showed up and attended the Idaho event.
7. As I was leaving, I took a few moments to respond to some questions from someone who attended my speech.
8. While responding to an inquiry, I noticed a meeting agenda showing Steve Wozniak as the conference keynote speaker.
9. I chose to stay and hear Steve Wozniak rather than go play golf and ended up seated next to his assistant, Julie, in the front row.

10. In a few short minutes of conversation, I got to know Julie, and we shared a basis of trust.

11. Julie introduced me to Steve. We had common points of interest as well as mutual friends.

12. I immediately emailed Steve and asked him to join our advisory board, which he accepted right away.

13. Steve showed up for me, and I showed up for him. I became CEO of Fusion-io, and Steve became my Chief Scientist.

If any link in the foregoing chain of events had been broken, Wozniak would have never joined Fusion-io. My guess is that Fusion-io would have still been successful; however, his influence and input in terms of marketing, sales, and technology has been invaluable.

Five Reasons to Get in Front of People

The experience above illustrates several important reasons to show up for people. If you show up to serve, show up to create top-of-mind awareness, show up to inspire mutual growth, show up to build relationships, and show up to exchange services, you will truly Up Your Game and lay the foundation for success.

Show Up to Serve

When you show up to meet with others, your efforts should always center around creating positive results, growth, and impact. In the game-changing connection described above, I showed up to a lunch meeting with a young lawyer because I wanted to serve him, and the ultimate result was beyond anything I could have hoped for. Are you seeing these opportunities? Are you expanding those with whom you come in contact? Is your first thought when attending a business meeting, "What can I do to help you?" Are you developing depth in your relationships that produces measured results? Can you trace the success in your own life and business to the influence and impact of others? Are you offering positive growth to others by way of your expertise and resources? Lastly, are you seeking associations that would be mutually beneficial, mutually satisfying, and mutually supportive?

Your desires to serve, fueled by a genuine curiosity and interest in people and their needs, can also be accomplished through technology platforms. In our busy day-to-day world, we may overlook the value of ping-ponging conversations we might have on various social media platforms. We may undervalue their ability to generate change or alter circumstances. We may feel intimidated by reaching out to those we do not know—especially those who are in leadership or who are well known. The key again is to "show up" consistently and personally to be known and get to know others. As people hear from you, see your name, see your company name, and recognize your brand, you become a resource and trusted ally.

Show Up to Create Top-of-Mind Awareness

Showing up is much more than just attending a conference or stopping by someone's office. It is also about creating top-of-mind awareness among respected peers. For example, my daughter's obstetrician, Tom, knew me to have a law background. He knew me to be a person of influence. And when his son-in-law had a need, I came to mind. In your business or trade, will people call you for advice? What problem or difficulty would prompt them to pick up the phone and call you? Have they seen you as a domain expert at events or online in ways and places that would inspire them to see you as a resource or leader?

More than ever before, we can use online tools to reach out and be present with others. Through emails, texts, Facebook, Instagram, LinkedIn, and Twitter, we can connect, share ideas, exchange resources, and offer support. As you "show up" online, you will build rapport and credibility by what you say and how you say it. This creates top-of-mind awareness as those you connect with become familiar with you and easily engage with you.

In networking, you are your product, and your reputation is your brand. To be successful as a leader with the power to influence people for good, you must grasp the concept that to have traction in people's lives they must picture your face, your skills, and your talent when specific needs arise. Your goal is to be on their minds when they scroll through their mental rolodex in search of a solution to a particular problem. Your impact is only as effective as this top-of-mind awareness. How can you increase your top-of-mind awareness in relationships? Show up. Be seen. Be engaged. Be engaging. Be willing to serve. Be present. Social media gives each of us an unparalleled opportunity to have our expertise and knowledge seen and be appreciated by thousands. Join LinkedIn groups, Google+, and Facebook pages where those of like mind can come to know you and the skill set you possess.

Speaking of people that showed up, I reflect on the cofounder of Microsoft, William Henry Gates III. In 1981, Bill Gates "showed up" at IBM, which resulted in an agreement with Big Blue that changed the course of the computer industry. I will delve into that important contract and connection elsewhere in this book in more detail, but it is important to note that Gates had created some important alliances within IBM. When IBM needed a disk operating system for their first business personal computer, Gates was only a phone call away. Gary Kildall, who had actually invented the first PC operating system at the Naval Research Laboratories, was IBM's first choice to supply the O.S. But when IBM showed up at Gary's offices in Monterey, California, Gary was enjoying a morning of flying his aircraft and failed to "show up" for at least the first part of this incredibly important meeting. Kildall did not get the contract, but Gates did. The agreement between Microsoft and IBM, wherein IBM licensed MSDOS is arguably the most valuable contract in the history of the world. It made Gates the wealthiest man on planet Earth. Gates showed up. Kildall did not.

Show Up to Inspire Mutual Growth

Today, with our twenty-first-century social media platforms, we are able to show up physically and digitally, as well. I show up every morning online via LinkedIn, Twitter, and Facebook with an inspirational thought for the day. Recently, I had occasion to speak with Mike Muhney, founder and former CEO of ACT Software, who built the earliest iteration of contact management software. During our conversation, he said something that really caught my attention—so I posted his statement on Facebook and got a multitude of "likes."

> *Facebook July 10, 2013* – Friends, great quote below. Had a terrific phone call today with the founder of ACT software. He and his team originated contact management software in the 80's. Now Mike is up to his next thing. As we discussed what keeps us both motivated, he said: "I choose to use success as a springboard, not a hammock." Awesomely said . . .

This is what I mean by showing up digitally. Let people know you are out there. Let people know that you are a domain expert in some way.

As a result of my Facebook post, a technologist by the name of Bob Sieger reached out and introduced me to a colleague of his in the recruiting industry. The net result is that we interviewed this young man for a job at HireVue. It all came about because Bob "liked" my Facebook post.

Recently, my son, David Eric Bradford, shared with me a terrific article from the *Harvard Business Review*. So I posted the following on LinkedIn and Twitter.

> From an HBR article shared with me by son David Eric: "A growing body of research suggests that the way to influence—and to lead—is to begin with warmth. Warmth is the conduit of influence."

That quote was liked and commented on by Bryan Schramm, a successful entrepreneur from Denver. Net Result: I am now serving on Bryan's advisory board for his fast-growing technology company.

Show Up to Build Relationships—One Contact at a Time

Finding relationship connections is a great foundation for business or personal relationships. But networking is done one event at a time, one contact at a time. As we talk about networking and connecting with people, it is significant to remember that connections begin with intersections. There is a point of contact at a specific place and time. To facilitate more connections and more networks, one has to actively engage in the process. This takes courage and tenacity. It takes a concerted effort over time.

This may sound daunting. When I start a task that seems especially intimidating, I remember a story of a courageous female bush pilot. As the story goes, while flying within the Arctic Circle, this bush pilot encountered bad weather. She had no option but to crash land her plane. With no means of transportation, she was desperate to get to a place of safety. Armed with a few supplies from the wreckage of the plane, she began to hike her way out. The nearest outpost was some 600 miles away. She knew the only way to survive was to make it to this station on foot. Determined, and with dwindling supplies, bad weather, dangerous conditions, and even frozen ground, she walked the 600 miles to her destination. When asked by the people in the hospital how she was able to overcome the brutal conditions and walk the 600 miles, her response was simple but deeply instructional: "I didn't walk 600 miles. I walked one mile, six hundred times."

Every great accomplishment begins with one step, then another, and another. Each step taken creates a greater distance traveled. Each step adds to the accomplishment. So it is with networking. Each step you take to connect with another individual adds value and strength of purpose. Never in the history of mankind have there been more tools at your disposal to build a well-organized network. Building a phenomenal network takes place one minute at a time, one contact at a time, one event at a time, one business card at a time, and one individual placed in one category at a time in your database.

Ray Kroc, founder of the McDonald's empire, said this: "The two most important requirements for major success are, first, being in the right place at the right time, and second, doing something about it." Consistently and purposefully showing up at physical and virtual events will help you meet other people who want to up their games, as well. Think on this: If you added just five people a day on LinkedIn, over a year's time you would create more than 1,500 new connections. Each connection offers multiple possibilities in business, relationships, and support. In fact, according to LinkedIn, my over 11,500 direct connections link me to over 25 million other professionals. In other words, for each direct contact I have on that platform, I am connected to roughly 2000 additional people. The small steps required to add one contact at a time can manifest great rewards down the road. That's why I have built more than 10,000 LinkedIn connections and have done it one at a time.

Show Up to Exchange Services

Recently, one of our great sales representatives for HireVue wrote the following to our company's sales organization. He arrived a day early to a conference that he was attending on behalf of Hire-Vue and went swimming with his family at the pool. After visiting with one of the fellow guests at the pool, he obtained a golden contact for HireVue. He later wrote the following as his checklist for attending a business conference:

> Get to event early to enjoy the resort with kids & wife = Check!
>
> Get a special rate and save HireVue $50/day = Check!
>
> Get a lead within the first hour of being here = priceless.

Hit the pool and gave a pitch while swimming in the pool and got a great lead! Let me remind you:

#ABN - Always be Networking! (a page out of David Bradford's book.)

Regards, Doug - Regional Sales Manager

Doug showed up and spoke up like Forest Gump on the park bench chatting with whomever passed by. "When you speak up," Doug added, "it can be to a potential friend, colleague, client, or employer. You will never know unless you ask."

Deborah Day once said: "Encourage, lift and strengthen one another. For the positive energy spread to one will be felt by us all. For we are connected, one and all." Reaching out to others with a genuine desire to help them accomplish *their* goals is the best way to succeed in your own life and relationships. In this respect, I like the concept of consultative selling, where 90 percent of your conversation with potential clients is about what *their* needs are. Once you really understand where the other person is coming from, the easier it will be to port your skill sets and expertise to help them resolve their problems.

Conclusion

I like the term "professional chain-links" to describe how seemingly random events can add up to rewarding, long-term connections. These are incidents or events that put you in close proximity to others. The more events that you do, the more often you "show up," and the more visible you are, the greater chance you have of upping your game with substantive interactions that form important professional chain-links. My game-changing experience was a direct result of showing up to serve, to create top-of-mind awareness, to inspire mutual growth, to build relationships, and to exchange services.

Are you showing up to Up Your Game?

CHAPTER 4 GAME PLAN

1. 90 percent of success in life comes from just showing up.

2. Show up in style. Stand out from the crowd when you attend an event. Brightly colored clothing, tastefully worn, can help make you memorable.

3. Show up with purpose. Go to receptions, conventions, and the like with the intent of seeing what you can do for others.

4. Show up on professional groups on LinkedIn, Google+, and the like, and actively post comments so people will keep you at the top of their minds.

5. Be the first person to arrive at an event. You will be able to more quickly judge how to navigate the situation.

6. The best two jobs I ever got occurred by simply walking into the business I was targeting. Sometimes, you simply have to show up and be bold!

PRINCIPLE 3: FOLLOW UP

Immediate follow-up is absolutely essential to stay top of mind, to stay in touch, to Up Your Game, and to be memorable. To me, the principle of follow-up is almost a lost art. I also think it is a matter of habit. Those that follow up quickly and memorably set aside a specific time each day to do it. Perhaps it is the last thing they do at night or the first thing they do in the morning. But they do it consistently and impressively, and they are the winners as a result.

I recently read some interesting statistics from a website aptly named "Follow Up Success" (followupsuccess.com).

Alan Underkofler is a social media strategist and the founder of Follow Up Success. On his site, he points out some sad but, in my experience, true statistics about the follow-up habits of salespeople. According to Alan, 48 percent of salespeople never follow up with a prospect; 25 percent of salespeople make a second contact and stop; and only 12 percent of salespeople make more than three contacts.

But note these following rather revealing stats that Alan included: 2 percent of sales are made on the first contact; 3 percent of sales are made on the second contact; 5 percent of sales are made on the third contact; 10 percent of sales are made on the fourth contact; and 80 percent of sales are made on the fifth to twelfth contact.

The conclusion is an easy one. *Follow up if you want to Up Your Game and close that sale.*

Recently, I gave a speech where one of the audience members heard me make reference to some work I had done in the past with software giant Oracle. Following the speech, a young man named Tanner boldly came up and introduced himself and told me his father was interviewing for a job with Oracle. I was busy responding to a lot of inquiries after my speech, so I did not have time to chat at that point. But when I arrived at home that night, this young man had taken the initiative to introduce me via email to his father. Because of the immediacy of the follow up, I remembered the young man very specifically and was able and willing to provide a broader introduction for his father to Oracle. Had the young man waited another 48 hours before pinging me back, there is a very real chance that I would not have had as distinct a memory of him, and my willingness to assist would have wavered.

By way of further illustration, several years earlier, I was at a speech delivered by Malcolm Gladwell, the famous author. During his speech, he mentioned a few things he admired about Google. Immediately following Malcolm's speech, I walked up to meet him and asked if he had ever met Eric Schmidt of Google in person or had been out to their headquarters in Mountain View, California. The answer was "no" but that he would like to someday.

That was on a Friday night. The next day (note that it's within my 24-hour rule) I penned the following to Malcolm:

Date: Mar 13, 2010

Dear Malcolm,

It was a rare privilege to meet you. I have been running my company, Fusion-io, based on some of the principles taken from Outliers. I had no idea you were going to be at the Sundance event sponsored by Credit Suisse—*so the timing was terrific.*

I want to follow up on something we discussed briefly:

Introduction to Eric Schmidt at Google—happy to do this. Eric and I have stayed close over the last ten years since our time of working together at Novell. Just let me know and I will open the door there.

Malcolm responded within 24 hours with a very kind note thanking me for the email and indicating he had enjoyed our meeting. He agreed to take me up on my offer and added that he thought Fusion-io "sounds really cool."

The point is this: Successful people respond and do it with immediacy. Malcolm is proof of that. Also, if I had waited a week to email Malcolm, there would have been at least an 80 or 90 percent chance of his saying, "Now, who was that guy, and where did I meet him?" But instead, we developed a relationship that has become very meaningful to me. In fact, at one point Mr. Gladwell was kind enough to introduce me to his book agent regarding this very book.

I am always amazed at how frequently people fail to follow up immediately on seemingly important connections. I make it a personal practice to respond within 24 hours to any important meeting or interaction. Those who take the time to get back with a sense of urgency can differentiate themselves in the marketplace.

Most people fail to follow up immediately. If you want to Up Your Game in life and business, then be one of the top five percent who gets back quickly and meaningfully. As you build your network, choose organizational tools that will help you follow up easily, efficiently, and with maximum impact. Doing so will allow you to blast through "Dunbar's Number"—the statistical ceiling of relationship impact.

To Enable Great Follow-Up, Choose Great Tools

It is easy to meet someone and make a good first impression. It is much harder to follow up meaningfully, keep promises, and stay in touch with your contacts. Fortunately, today's world of technology and social media gives one an unprecedented ability to connect with others and follow up.

My experience is that only by staying in touch over the long term can one yield the most prolific results. When I give speeches, I enjoy picking out a couple of people out of the crowd that obviously don't know each other. I introduce the two individuals to one another in front of the audience and get them chatting and asking each other questions about their respective backgrounds. I, then, make this important point . . . You never know what contact you might make at church, school, or business that might be a real key to your successful future. I invite all at these events to exchange contact information, follow up with each other, and stay in touch.

To be a champion at follow-up, you need to choose current tools to organize your network in terms of ease, efficiency, and impact. These tools will maximize your ability to follow up and stay connected.

Choose Your Tools Wisely

Remember, a tool is only a vehicle to facilitate a principle. Thus, it behooves you to find the tool or medium that best fits your personality and audience. Whatever tool you employ, be it your email, texting, Facebook, LinkedIn, Foursquare, Twitter, Instagram, or

Google+, the goal is to create relationships that are meaningful, deep, and actionable.

Many of you reading this book are part of what author and educator Marc Prensky has described as the "last pre-Internet generation." We are in a transition phase and are moving to a wholly new Internet generation—*a group of people that do not know what life was like before the Web.* My 16 grandchildren are part of that new generation. But the point is that the Internet has provided a plethora of revolutionary tools to connect!

In this book, I spend a lot of time discussing social media applications, like Facebook and LinkedIn, because they are the most current organizational tools. However, it is essential to note that while the Up Principles are timeless, the mediums of distribution will always be changing. I expect that in short order these technologies will be followed by more innovations that will force us to stretch our thinking and our processes. In my view, Facebook will be fundamentally different in ten years from what it is today and might not even be the massively influential medium we currently utilize daily.

As you meet people and manage your interactions with them with any application, you will need to organize your contacts, incrementally invest in them, create and maintain credibility, and give without getting. *This all happens through following up.* As you plan for growth in number and depth of your network, find tools that can support your database in terms of ease, efficiency, and impact.

Your Platform Must Be Easy

Every contact management program exists to organize and optimize your database of people. SalesForce.com, for example, has built a big business on offering such tools to salespeople. Social media tools are no different. LinkedIn, Facebook, and other platforms can help you optimize your relationships to have the greatest impact on those relationships. The value proposition is to choose your tools and employ them in ways that harness your people easily and effectively. Learn how to cultivate the network for maximum efficiency so that when you need to call upon it, it is ready to respond. As Ken Blanchard, the noted author and business strategist, said: "None of us is as smart as all of us."

Choose tools that utilize your email contacts. Every great oak tree starts from a single seed. The same is true with any great network. Undoubtedly, you already have a database of contacts in an email address book. It is probably larger than you think. All of the popular social networking platforms, such as Twitter, Facebook, and LinkedIn, allow you to quickly import your contacts directly from email platforms such as Yahoo, Gmail, or Microsoft Outlook. If no direct import exists for your address book, there is another alternative.

Several years ago, I discovered something called a CSV file. CSV stands for "Comma Separated Values." I still don't know exactly what that means, but it allows you to export all of your email contacts into one file. You can open and read a CSV file on your computer or import it into any of the common social media platforms of the day.

After you import your contacts into a given social media platform, you will be asked which of your connections you'd like to invite to connect with you on that platform. You do not need to invite every contact on every platform. Typically, personal friends are a natural fit for Facebook. Business colleagues are a much more likely fit for LinkedIn. Naturally, some of your connections will be both business and personal friends.

Some people hesitate to import their entire address book from Gmail, Yahoo, or Outlook into the invitation system of a given social or professional network because they want to avoid "spamming" their contacts. It is important to remember that even if you import your entire address book, you can still choose which of your imported contacts actually get invited.

Recently, I launched a new website called DavidBradford.com. Using CSV capabilities built into all of my social media platforms along with my email databases from Yahoo to Gmail to Outlook, I created a single database of all of my connections. It numbered over 22,000—but because I had taken the time to categorize my connections in each of my separate data sources, I was able to go back and target a subset of that 22,000 for purposes of sending a broad email announcing the launch of DavidBradford.com. It avoided spamming a group of folks who were not as well known to me.

Choose tools that you can use easily on a daily basis. As you look at which tools or mediums to invest your time in, focus on one or two technologies that you can easily use every day. Facebook is easy. That is why Facebook users have such a broad age range. Facebook easily allows you to connect to people personally. With the ability to "Friend" others and "Find" old contacts, you can rapidly expand your network in a short time. If a program is difficult to utilize or challenging to set up, then you will find yourself losing the drive to add contacts to your network. That stack of business cards on your desk from last month's "meet and greet" will collect dust. You will not take the steps regularly to capture the leads and place them in your resource funnel. If you choose a platform that is easy and user-friendly, the process will be fast to utilize, easy to maintain on a daily basis, and quick to show growth in networking numbers.

Once you are on those platforms and begin networking, be systematic in growing your network from there. Every time you go to a business conference, gather a bunch of business cards. *Remember, the key to successful networking is not the number of cards you give out but rather the number of cards you collect.* Once you have someone's contact information, you are in the driver's seat. You have the ability to add that person to whatever network you prefer. I have tried to make it a regular practice that within 24 hours of any initial meeting, I send an invitation to join me on one of my social media platforms along with a personalized note to do so. Again, immediate follow-up is important so that your persona will be fresh in the minds of your contacts when they receive your request to connect.

Here's another little secret to help you grow your online network and presence. Go online and study the networks of your most connected and most successful friends. See who they are linked to. Create strategic connections by using personalized invitations and comments. Even if you only add one new person each day, you will find your number of connections growing quickly as you are exposed to new pools of people. Stay committed to adding people to your network. But again, make it personal. I just sent an email to a noted author. But rather than just sending him one of those "I'd like to add you to my Professional Network" preconfigured blasts, I wrote the following:

"Dear Nolan, Congratulations on your terrific success with your recent book. I loved the part where you spoke about Steve Jobs' early successes . . . as well as his failures. You have achieved much in your career. I have been CEO of several tech companies that have done reasonably well. We have 22 mutual connections on LinkedIn, and I would like to add you to my network. Kind Regards, David."

Find areas of commonality with those with which you wish to connect. It will engender a feeling of trust and will exponentially increase your success at connecting with people you may never have met.

Note that there are times and circumstances where I feel people can, and should, reach out to connect with someone whom they may not have met previously. If done with thought and class, the chances of a great new connection are greatly enhanced. But the key is to find areas of commonality and trust. Note that in the invitation to connect, above, I refer to our mutual work as a

CEO, our mutual previous encounter with Steve Jobs, and our 22 mutual LinkedIn connections.

Your Platform Must Be Efficient

In selling real estate, the adage is, "Location, location, location." In networking, my adage is, "Categorization, categorization, categorization." This is where most people fall short in their capabilites of upping their games and becoming great networkers. If you will thoughtfully use the advice below, you will be more successful than 95 percent of the networkers out there.

Every network I create is organized by groups and categories. This is the most efficient way to follow up with people I know. This is the only way to harness your people, your pools of skills and talent, and your resources in a focused manner. Every busy person can consistently reach out and leverage connections if he or she will categorize his or her database for effective campaigns down the road.

Whether you want to communicate with 100 CEOs or 500 salespeople, categorizing your contacts is essential. I do this on Facebook, my business Outlook account, and my email accounts. For example, Yahoo, Gmail, Outlook, and other email databases allow you to assign any number of categories to your contacts. You can then sort through your address book by category and presto! You have a quick and efficient way to communicate with a targeted distribution list.

Adding a contact without categorizing is a waste of time. Please understand this. If I add a contact without identifying and purposing our relationship and our common interests, then I lose any possible outcomes. How often are you adding contacts to your database (feeling proud of yourself for growing your network), yet never identifying what purpose those individuals will play in your life or your business down the road? Simply adding a random name and number to your phone does not a strategic alliance make. How do you see yourself working with these people? What skills do they have? With what groups in your lists do they align? Why would you ever reconnect with these people, and why would they ever reconnect with you?

Personalize Your Connections

Be sure to personalize your approach when adding contacts to your database, whether it is Twitter, Facebook, your email database, or LinkedIn. One of the keys to successful communication in any type of social media is to personalize your approach. People matter. This is foundational. They must feel as though they matter to you. People don't care how much you know until they know how much you care. You show concern and care for people when you take the time and effort to get to know them, understand what makes them tick, and ask how they have become the people they are today.

Every individual has a unique emotional DNA. If you ever care to do business with a person, it is important that you get to know him or her at more than a superficial level. With today's tools of social media and Google search, you can quickly and almost effortlessly get to know people's likes and dislikes and what motivates them. Knowing them deeper and sharing common interests with them engenders trust. As Steven M.R. Covey teaches, "When trust exists, business accelerates." Your genuine interest shows others that you are credible and trustworthy.

Let's review an example. Let's say you add Mary as a new Facebook friend. You know Mary as a practicing attorney from your church congregation who likes to play golf. She also happens to be a cousin. When you add Mary to your network, the system will pop up with your preconfigured categories and allow you the ease of simply checking the boxes: attorney, church, family, golf.

LinkedIn offers you the ability to access your contacts in a number of different ways: by location, job title, or company name, among other things. Let me provide some illustrations.

When you go to the top of your LinkedIn page, click on the icon that says "Network." Glance down and you will see ways to filter your connections by title, company, or location. Then you can select how to sort those connections by when you last conversed with them on LinkedIn, or their name, or the date of when you connected with them.

For example, I recently filtered my contacts by their job titles. If you click on that category, you will see the people to whom you are connected by title. So looking at my personal LinkedIn account as I write this, I see I am currently connected to 336 people who have "CEO" in their titles. I have also sorted those CEOs in terms of when I connected to them.

By way of another example, I filtered by company name and discovered that I have 48 people on LinkedIn with whom I am directly connected that work at IBM. I also sorted through them and found out when I connected with each of them, from the most recent connection to the oldest.

By sorting through and studying your connections, you can get to know the who, what, where, and how of your contacts, allowing for more personalized interactions. Consistent, strategic categorization gives you a powerful tool for quickly connecting to a specific demographic to get answers to questions or follow up. Word to the wise, here: When you are sending out an email correspondence to an entire distribution list, be sure to place all of your addresses in the "bcc" field. Put yourself in the "To: Address Line." It is almost always better to have all addresses in the bcc field to avoid revealing email addresses to others.

Once you have addressed your email to your preset group, always go back through the bcc field and filter out the people you do not wish to include from that group on this particular mailing. For example, let's say that I am inviting folks to play in a golf tournament with me. I add my "golf" group from my preset categories into my bcc field and draft the following notice to all golfing friends: "I have a tremendous golf opportunity for someone, but I need a quick reply. I am looking to fill out a team for a golf tourney March 10/14 at the world-famous Pinehurst resort." This may not be an invitation that I necessarily want to send to everyone on my golf list.

Before I hit send, I quickly peruse my bcc field and delete anyone who would not value that particular communication, including my boss and anyone else I do not wish to know about my golf outing. Deleting contacts from the bcc field will not delete them from my "golf" group permanently—it will only delete them from the email I am in the process of sending.

In a nutshell, categorizing will:

- Save you time when sending out messages.
- Allow you to follow up.
- Target a specific segment of your database.
- Allow dragging and dropping of an entire category directly into your address space.
- Allow for quick and easy follow-up with a specific group.
- Target the exact people with whom you want to share specific content or events.

Let me share an experience from several years ago that demonstrates the power of categorization. It references specifically the aforementioned golf outing at Pinehurst, which resulted in a wonderful opportunity to work with the great David Checketts. David is chairman and CEO of the Legends—a combined entity owned by the New York Yankees, the Dallas Cowboys, and Dave himself, who is the former President of Madison Square Garden, the New York Knicks, and leading American soccer team Real Salt Lake.

Early in 2011, I was searching for people to play in a golf tournament with me in Pinehurst, North Carolina. My regular partners were unable to attend, so I needed to fill some open slots on my team. I went to my Yahoo database and identified the categories that I had created that contained all of my connections who were interested in golf. I tapped out an email on my computer and sent it out to everyone in two categories: Sports and Golf.

Friday, February 25, 2011

Subject: Urgent Golf Opportunity

I have a tremendous golf opportunity for someone, but I need a quick reply. I am looking to fill out a team for a golf tourney March 10-14 at the world-famous Pinehurst resort. This tourney is a blast. Liberty Mutual is the sponsor for the competition to be held in North Carolina.

Please let me know if you have an interest in joining me.

Warm Regards, David B

A response came back from Dave Checketts that read:

Monday, February 28, 2011

David,

So I have a deal for you . . . I will come and play and lend my extremely valuable 18 handicap, with excellent putting skills . . .

All you have to do is look at a sports and media investment fund.

We will be buying distressed NBA and Major League Baseball assets, as well as Premier League and other international sports assets.

I have kept the group small with guys I know well and trust. I would like very much for you to consider it.

Best, dwc

I was excited and flattered that Dave Checketts was willing to come and play golf with me. I had seen or spoken to Dave only rarely in the previous 25 years. We had met during my early days at Novell at about the same time Dave was starting his career in the NBA. Over time and through the power of email and social media, I had stayed in touch with Dave. When the time was right, we were able to meet together in a synergistic way.

Dave and I met for a couple of days of wonderful golf down at Pinehurst. While there, Dave explained that he was in the process of raising a $250 million fund to invest in professional sports franchises. Naturally, one of the keys to creating a successful fund is having a series of anchor investors. Dave saw me as someone with a large network who might be instrumental in introducing him to qualified participants in his new fund. I would never have reconnected with Dave but for the small step I had taken years earlier to put Mr. Checketts in my "Sports" category. As a direct result, both Daves were able to Up Their Games.

Let me share a bit more about harnessing the efficiency of a categorized network. Again, using the power of categorization, I identified a number of high net worth venture capitalists and investment bankers located in Northern California who might have an interest in what Dave Checketts was doing. I turned to my Yahoo database, pulled up the "VC" and "I-Banker" categories, and quickly targeted twenty or so of them located in the Bay area. With the help of my Yahoo database, supplemented by my Facebook connections, within just a matter of hours I was able to pull together fourteen meetings over two days in San Francisco, Palo Alto, and Menlo Park with some of the most financially well-positioned people on planet Earth.

These meetings included a rather exciting meeting with Frank Quattrone and his team at Qatalyst Partners. I have known Frank since the late 80's, but our interactions have been intermittent over the years. However, because Frank was in my "I-Banker" category, it was much easier to remember and connect with him when the time was right. Dave Checketts and I met with him in his magnificent offices overlooking the beautiful San Francisco Bay. Mr. Quattrone was generous to give us nearly an hour and a half of his valuable time. I learned later just how valuable his time was that day. In leaving, Frank and his partner humbly apologized that they could not spend more time with us. They mentioned they were in the middle of another matter. Less than two hours after leaving Frank's office, the news broke that Quattrone and his group had just represented National Semiconductor in the $6.5 billion negotiation with Texas Instruments, wherein Frank achieved a 78 percent premium on the merger between the two companies on behalf of his client!

Frank Quattrone is someone who follows up and follows through. He is a shining example of someone who has built and maintained a powerful network of knowledgeable and successful tech CEOs around the globe. This is something that plays to his advantage daily. In the hallowed halls of investment banking, Frank is probably the most trusted mergers and acquisitions professional anywhere in the world. He advised Eric Schmidt and Google at the time Microsoft tried to buy out Google. A key factor in Frank's success is that he is a networker above most networkers. He also keeps his commitments. When Dave Checketts and I set a meeting time with Frank that morning, he could have easily called and said, "Hey Dave, I am in the middle of an important matter. Can we reschedule?" To Frank's credit and credibility, he followed through on our meeting.

All of these connections and exchanges were made possible and expedited because of the efficient network organization that had been built over many years. Had I not built and maintained a global network of contacts identifying key groups of constituents, this outcome would have taken months and perhaps may not have occurred at all. I cannot emphasize enough the need for an efficient method of managing and harnessing your database. In optimum times, it is your greatest strength, allowing you to Up Your Game by following up meaningfully and efficiently within minutes.

Your Platform Is Your Vehicle of Impact When Properly Organized

Whether you are recruiting for a position, looking for talent, needing a question answered, or merely inviting people to a golf tournament, setting up your categories is a powerful way to leverage your network. If you have not begun putting your contacts into categories, get on it. Now.

As I stated earlier in this book, *an uncategorized contact is a wasted contact.* Only by categorizing are you able to launch with impact into a specific sector of people. Thus, your platform or application, because of its efficiency, will become your vehicle of impact that can catapult your ventures quickly and powerfully.

To the extent that it might be useful to you, here are the categories that I have created for my Yahoo email database in alphabetical order. You may wish to do the same or something similar—but customize your categories for your own purposes. Again, think *impact.* What groups of people do I want to impact? What groups or pools of people impact me, my industry, my family, or my goals? Organizing your pools of impact will greatly expedite your success when you have a need or when you have a solution and will allow you to follow up and stay in touch in a powerful way.

- *Accountants*
- *Angel Investors*
- *Arizona Contacts*
- *Attorneys*
- *Bankers*
- *Buyout Funds*
- *BYU*
- *Celebrities*
- *CEOs*

- *CIO's*
- *Clients*
- *Doctors*
- *Educators*
- *Entrepreneurs*
- *European Contacts*
- *Executives*
- *Facebook (People that work at Facebook corporate)*
- *Family*
- *Friends*
- *Funding Universe (Another company I started)*
- *Fusion-io*
- *General Counsels*
- *Golf Friends*
- *Google Friends*
- *Government Connections*
- *Harbor Hills Ward (Members of a church congregation to which I belonged)*
- *Huntsman Supporters*
- *Investment Bankers*
- *IBM Friends*
- *Insurance Industry*
- *International Connections*
- *Judicial*
- *Kids (My children and their wives)*
- *LDS Friends*
- *LDS.Biz*
- *LDS OC (Mormon friends in Orange County, California)*
- *Major Accounts*

- *Marketing Friends*
- *Matchbin*
- *Millenniata*
- *MLM (My acquaintances in the network marketing world)*
- *Mutual (A youth organization in my church)*
- *Novell Friends*
- *OC Contacts*
- *OCMA (An Orange County Management society for which I was once president)*
- *Precinct 42 (a local political subdivision)*
- *Real Estate Friends*
- *Red Lodge (Acquaintances from my old hometown in Montana)*
- *Romney Supporters (A big list—I was a national co-chair for Romney for President)*
- *Salespeople*
- *Sports*
- *St. George*
- *Technologists*
- *Texas*
- *Travel*
- *Utah Tech Council*
- *UVU Board (I used to be on the Board of Trustees of Utah Valley University)*
- *VC's*
- *VC Investors (These are people that invest in VC funds)*
- *VIEW (Those people who are associated with Dr. Linda Bradford's company, Virtual Immersive Educational World)*

As mentioned earlier, you can separate and identify specific groups of people within LinkedIn based on the predefined categories provided by LinkedIn. There are roughly 150 categories.

They align with industry types such as accounting, banking, insurance, law, real estate and venture capital.

Hopefully this will provide you with an idea of how quickly and efficiently you can connect with people in various industries when needed once your network is built up. Throughout the book, I have given you actual examples, as I am doing here, for the purpose of showing you how doable this process is and the specifics of putting it into action. Anyone can do this. Smart networkers will take the time to do it and continue to do it as they grow their network. Whether you choose Instagram, Yahoo, LinkedIn, Foursquare, Facebook, Twitter, or a future platform with even more innovations and bells and whistles, your platform, organized this way, will be your vehicle to impact and inform the masses. This is how and where you harness and impact your audience.

Blow Through Dunbar's Number

There is a theory that, in social networks, the optimum number of connections is 150. This theory is called "Dunbar's Number."

The so-called rule of 150 asserts that the size of a genuine social network is limited to about 150 members. The rule arises from cross-cultural studies in sociology and especially anthropology of the maximum size of a village (most reasonably understood today as an eco-village). It is theorized in evolutionary psychology that the number may be some kind of limit of average human ability to recognize members and track emotional facts about all members of a group.[1]

Taking the time today to create specific categories within your email or social networking platforms permits you to become a

---

1   See Wellman, B. (2012). "Is Dunbar's number up?" *British Journal of Psychology* 103 (2): 174-176, and Gladwell, M. (2000). *The Tipping Point: How Little Things Make a Big Difference.* Little, Brown and Company, pp. 177-181, 185-186.

juggernaut of networking, because you can truly stay in touch and follow up when necessary with not hundreds but thousands. As mentioned earlier, the vast majority of people shy away from what they perceive as a tedious task. *Those who have the patience and the perseverance to categorize have a distinct competitive advantage in the marketplace.*

The goal of this principle is to follow up and stay in touch effectively and efficiently. In the fall of 2008, as I had recently joined Fusion-io myself on a full-time basis, I began searching for a capable executive assistant. I had been connected to Sarah Elwell DeLange on Facebook. We had a couple of mutual friends. As I perused her profile, I noted that Sarah had worked at the headquarters of Marriott Corporation back in Maryland. I also noticed that one of her contacts, her sister Shannon, had also worked as an executive assistant at Marriott and was now working in Utah as a CEO assistant. Reaching out to Shannon as she accepted my friend request, I inquired about her work at the Marriott Corporation.

Shannon explained that she had been the executive assistant to Steve Marriott, a Senior VP for the company, back at Marriott headquarters. She also told me about her current work assisting another Utah-based company, where she was presently at the time employed by the president of that company. A phone call ensued, interviews followed, and I hired Shannon. In my 30-plus years in the industry, Shannon is definitely among the best of all the assistants I have ever worked with. She is capable, hardworking, and a consummate networker herself—even responding to emails after 11:00 p.m. For Shannon and me, it was a match made in heaven that was made entirely possible from a Facebook connection.

Here is the body of an email I received from Shannon's sister, who followed up with me shortly after I hired Shannon.

Congratulations . . . on reaching a milestone on Facebook at 5000 friends on Facebook. You're an incredible networker. I told Shannon she has officially met her match =)

Your platform application or applications will be your vehicle of impact. You will impact others, and others will positively impact you and support you in having greater success through their gifts and skills. You can't very well impact the masses if you don't have a listening audience. So follow up, follow up, and follow up again.

Your network is your audience. Your network is your resource pool. Your network is "the masses." Your platform of choice is simply the vehicle to stay in touch. Whichever platform you choose, keep at the forefront of your mind to always be planning, always be organizing, and always be prioritizing so you can more effectively Up Your Game by staying in touch.

Are you immediately following up to Up Your Game easily, effectively, and with impact?

CHAPTER 5 GAME PLAN

1. Many people will "show up," but precious few follow up. So follow up, and do it now!

2. Be personal in everything you do. When you send a LinkedIn or Facebook connection request, personalize your request.

3. You should and can always be networking. Master networkers are individuals who realize that networking is a life skill, not just something you use when you want something for yourself. In order to succeed at building your network, it is important to show up at events, make strong connections, follow up, and keep in touch.

4. Follow up within 24 hours of any significant meeting by sending your new acquaintance an email, a text, an Instagram add, a LinkedIn request, a tweet, or a Facebook friend request.

5. From time to time, people *think* to contact a friend about the loss of his job or think to congratulate another buddy on his latest adventure or a sister's move or a friend's graduation. Yet, these fleeting thoughts go through our minds, and we miss the opportunity to act and connect. The difference makers in the world are those people who actually follow up and take action on those positive thoughts.

6. Use Hootsuite, Everyone Social, Eloqua, or other contact management software to follow up and ping your database at least once a month.

PRINCIPLE 4: LINK UP

I n June of 2013, my wife and I found ourselves at one of the best three-day events we have ever attended. Mitt Romney hosted a conference of 200 executives in Park City, Utah, to discuss and find solutions for our nation's most perplexing problems. To Mitt's credit, he not only invited a select group of Republican leaders to the confab, but also invited leading Democratic thought leaders like David Axelrod, President Obama's senior campaign strategist for Obama 2012, along with Antonio Villaraigosa, Democratic Mayor of Los Angeles. Mitt knows how to link up with people on more than a superficial level . . . and to do so with people across the entire political spectrum. I was wowed by Romney's ability to overlook not just petty but also substantive political differences and be willing to connect at a deep level with smart people regardless of their political affiliations. He also described his personal philosophy when connecting with others when he remarked, *"The currency of life is friendships."*

Cindy Crawford, former supermodel and one who has built a rather remarkable mini-empire around her personal brand, was the first speaker at the event. One of her comments resonated. She said, "Always ask yourself: 'How can I connect with others? You can learn something from everyone!'" I was very impressed with Cindy's determination to link up and learn from others.

Every business transaction has a basis in a personal relationship, so it is important to connect with people on a personal level. After all, people matter. As Steve Jobs stated, "It's not the tools that you have faith in—tools are just tools. They work, or they don't work. It's people you have faith in or not." By being curious, building win-win relationships, connecting on multiple platforms, and connecting personally and authentically, you will be poised to up your business game in significant ways and make a strong impact on those around you.

So how are you supposed to link up in order to Up Your Game? Here are my suggestions:

Be Curious

I am struck by the power of simply being curious and how that interest in others can drive important relationships that matter not just today but 20, 30, and 40 years down the road. Several years ago, I reconnected with someone I had not seen in over thirty years—Paul Toscano. I had journeyed to downtown Salt Lake City to attend a meeting in one of the high-rise buildings there. After finishing my meeting, I was descending in an elevator. It stopped at floor six. I glanced up to see who was getting on the elevator. Behind the individual, I saw a sign. It read: "Law Offices of Paul James Toscano." I quickly remembered my friend from years earlier and, in a moment of impulse, jumped off the elevator to see if it was the same individual I had known years previously.

I quietly approached the door to Paul's office and stood in the doorway waiting for Paul to cast a glance my way. Eventually, he looked over and, after a moment, a look of recognition covered his face. We embraced and began to excitedly chatter away, the thirty-plus years quickly melting away. At one point in the conversation, Paul was kind enough to congratulate me on "my many successes in the computer industry." And then he said something that really caught my attention:

"David, I always knew you would be successful." I was stunned for a bit and did not know how to reply to such a statement. After a moment, I fumbled a reply along the lines of, "Paul, what ever made you think that?"

His reply was revelatory to me and relevant to this book: "David, it was your *curiosity* that made me know you would be successful in life. You were always the most curious eighteen-year-old in the dorms. You were interested in everyone and everything they were doing."

Sometimes we become intimidated by overthinking the process. If you want to increase your affection for people and have more impact, get interested! It's that easy. How do you learn to genuinely connect with people? How do you learn to extend yourself, your interest, and your compassion for those around you and warm up so they feel your personality? My belief is that your love of people comes only after your curiosity about them begins. That's when you can begin to step it up.

In a February 2013 article in Forbes magazine entitled "Things Leaders Do," we learn that great managers "ask questions and seek counsel all the time." From the outside, it appears they know everything but "inside, they have a deep thirst for knowledge and constantly are on the lookout to learn new things." In other words . . . they are curious.

Connecting, relating, having top-of-mind status with others, creating a following—it's all about feeling, sincere curiosity, real emotion, trust, loyalty, and real interest. When you combine genuine interest in people with technology that can duplicate your message, disseminate your data, and create reciprocal interaction, a hundred doors of opportunity open to you. Let me offer a word of caution here. If you blast your email base with non-feeling spam, those same hundred doors will slam shut.

It does not require an advanced degree or a new lifestyle, just a simple commitment to being curious about people and genuinely learning to enjoy them.

Let me share with you a discussion I had at my bank a few years ago. After waiting in line for the teller, he waved me over to his window, and I placed my wallet on the counter. I retrieved my identification and shuffled through my banking items. The gentleman, who looked to be about forty years old, greeted me with a pleasantry and quickly commenced to process the transaction.

"Galactic Networks?" he asked, flipping my bankcard around to display the company name. (I give the teller an "A" for curiosity!)

"Yes, that's one of my businesses," I explained. "It's my parent company for Linking Universe, which is like LinkedIn built into Facebook."

"What's LinkedIn?" he asked, his pen making sweeping marks across the deposit slip as he talked.

I wasn't certain I understood his question. Had he never heard of LinkedIn?

I explained further, "It's a Facebook for business professionals. Are you a Facebooker?"

His answer to my question gave me all of the information I needed to know.

"No, I never really got into that social networking thing. Most of my friends do it, but I could never really get interested."

His inability to "get interested" in other people, innovative technology, and even what his friends were involved in painted a mental image of a dead-end sign. His interest level mirrored his fruition level in his life. If he chose not to change his trajectory, he would never lead a bigger life.

JC Penney, who founded the first department store in America (in the small town of Kemmerer, Wyoming), said this about interest and engagement:

"Show me a stock clerk with big dreams and specific goals, and I will show you a man that will have an impact on the world; show me a man with no dreams, and I will show you a stock clerk."

As I left the bank that day, I realized this 40-year-old bank teller may end up a 60-year-old bank teller. Or, as technology races faster and faster, this 40-year-old bank teller may be left on the side of the cyber-highway due to his lack of interest in linking up with people and making substantial business connections.

Whether it is technology or relationships themselves that require us to step out of our comfort zones, we will see rapid growth take place in our individual and professional confidence levels if we invest in those areas and push ourselves to be better and more effective.

Build Win-Win Relationships

Contrary to the phrase, "It's not personal, it's just business," business is always about people. When choosing a product, making a financial decision, or signing a long-term contract, value will always be given to the business that has developed a personal relationship and loyalty with the customer. *These connections need to start long before the customer needs something.* Indeed, real connecting is a continuous long-term proposition that is about positive win-win relationships.

As mentioned earlier, a road sign I saw some years ago read: "Every business relationship has its basis in a personal relationship." If that is true, and I firmly believe it is, we should be doing everything we can on a daily basis to secure and expand our personal relationships. If done with genuine interest and sincerity, customer loyalty will be a common denominator in every area.

People can flourish or flounder in their career aspirations based on how they connect, nurture, and expand their professional networks. As I reflect on my career in business and most recently in my roles as CEO of Fusion-io and HireVue, I recognize that my relationships and personal connections have been the fuel that has driven part of the engine of these companies. As said by Louis Gerstner, former IBM CEO, "Computers are magnificent tools for the realization of our dreams, but no machine can replace the human spark of spirit, compassion, love, and understanding."

I am not a computer scientist by training. And yet, my career has been linked to technology. I am not the smartest guy in the room, yet I, as an average lawyer having grown up in one of the smallest towns imaginable, came to run a company voted the "Most Innovative in the World." The secret? Business is personal.

As I connect the dots from year to year, from opportunity to opportunity, it becomes obvious that the opportunities I have been given are attributable to relationships that have been grown or established through simple interactions via technology. The fuel has been my love of people; technology has simply been the means to communicate with them.

One of my goals in writing this book was to explain how I create relationships in business and how, among other things, they helped me build a billion-dollar valuation for a company that had been shipping products for less than three years. That type of transformation, that type of elevation of a business or product, is uncommon. The road map, however, can be duplicated. Hopefully you will be able to see in my life some "lessons learned" that can be utilized as a training ground for your own adventures. They start and end with linking up with people on a deep level. I also hope that you hear in my words the gratitude I feel for those who've connected with me. This book is a story of mutual successes *with* the help of social media, my business colleagues, and innovative technologists.

One example of this is HireVue's former Director of Social Media, Erin Schurtz. When it came to hiring someone to drive our social media for HireVue, I wanted to find someone who had great experience using Facebook, as well as experience utilizing LinkedIn. A year or more earlier, as I was serving on the Romney National Finance Committee, I had met a young man named Brian Henderson. At that time, Brian had introduced me to his friend Erin, a social media guru with a six-year history in the recruiting and staffing industry. Erin and I went to lunch, and I was immediately impressed. Erin had started a completely web-based game show called the "Mormon Bachelorette" that had done so well, she was able to sell the rights to ABC. Erin had become an expert at utilizing social media to expand the footprint of her idea and engage the masses in participating in the online YouTube voting process. She was an avid Facebooker and understood how to create a buzz.

Fast forward now to HireVue and its search for a social media expert. Some time had passed, and Erin was now working for one of the world's top public relation firms. She was doing social media and marketing for them. The Mormon Bachelorette was still ongoing at the time. I reached out to Erin, telling her about HireVue and sharing my vision as to how that was a perfect fit for her background in social media and recruiting. We were fortunate that Erin caught the vision of the Talent Interaction Platform HireVue advances. The results have been so exceptional that recently HireVue was actually ranked higher than LinkedIn in terms of its social media profile. Every week Erin sends out a series of links and tweets that every employee in our company (nearly 200 team members) re-tweets, posts on LinkedIn, or recommends on Facebook. That's today's method of communication. If you're not seen on Facebook, LinkedIn, Twitter, Google+,

Pinterest, etc., you're losing out on a lot of opportunity. When people see that your company is being mentioned in the blogosphere, highlighted in key industry articles, and showing up on LinkedIn, Facebook, and Twitter, then they know you are part of a "happening" company. That has been a big benefit for HireVue, because when our sales force goes to call on prospective customers, they already know the company. As I was told recently: "Oh yeah, I see you guys out there all the time."

Erin's talent now opens doors for an entire company through her skills with technology. Social media gives us marketing power for our salespeople. Our credibility as a company and our consistent quality and performance then open more doors—and social media keeps them open.

These results for HireVue were all started by my friendship with Brian. As stated earlier, every business transaction (or quality hire) has its basis in a personal relationship. As an epilogue to this story, as I was putting the finishing touches on this book, I got a call out of the blue from Brian telling me about a new company he joined. He asked me to endorse their company to a potential funding source. Naturally, I reciprocated Brian's earlier kindness.

Connect Multiple Times

The best business is done through connecting—not just one time, but multiple times. In my mind, the value of networking is connecting with an extended ecosystem of people with similar pursuits and interests that support and sustain one another over time. That's where that genuine feeling, trust, and support come in. To grow your ecosystem, you must sustain it with caring and service; otherwise, it will die on the vine. Relationships require nurturing. As one of the leading venture capitalists in the world told me: "David, the word 'networking' understates what you do. What you do is build lasting relationships."

As we previously discussed, networking is doing everything you can on a regular basis to secure and expand your personal relationships in order to facilitate the likelihood for mutual success.

Connect on Multiple Platforms

Linking up with others in a personal way enables you to Up Your Game. Let me share with you the various social media platforms I use and why.

LinkedIn

My favorite place to network online for business is clearly LinkedIn. My test for any social or professional network is this: Am I driven to go there essentially every day? Four years ago, LinkedIn did not provide enough valuable information to create a compelling daily value proposition. But the team at LinkedIn has really stepped up their game. I find it more valuable than reading the *Wall Street Journal*. Today LinkedIn has more than a quarter of a billion users. If you want to link up in the world of business, use LinkedIn. LinkedIn provides a powerful set of tools allowing you to reach like-minded and well-connected professionals.

Essentially, LinkedIn provides its users the ability to link up and stay in touch with the people that can help advance their careers. It provides a platform allowing you to create an online professional profile that can highlight your career, your business, or your job search. LinkedIn Recruiter also provides great tools for companies to find talent.

I use LinkedIn to:

- Build a brand either for myself or my companies.
- Join groups of like-minded professionals—I belong to roughly twenty LinkedIn groups.
- Share quotes or thoughts on business that I think will help others.
- Comment on others' posts.

- Wish "Happy Birthday" to specific connections.

- Congratulate people on new jobs or promotions.

- Find the right person at a target company, like someone in business development, human resources, or sales.

- Get a reference from past professional colleagues.

- Endorse others and provide specific written recommendations on their work or character.

- Others like to search for jobs. There are important job postings on LinkedIn. One of the cool benefits of LinkedIn is that it enables you to find jobs you were not necessarily looking for.

Here are several ways that I harness the power of LinkedIn—methods that I believe to be underutilized by many:

Study the LinkedIn profile of target contacts carefully. Understand what schools they went to, the books they like, groups they have joined, endorsements or recommendations they have received, people who influence them, and companies they follow. Your goal should be to find what interests them—not necessarily you. After studying their profiles carefully, think of ways you can help them. Then use the power of LinkedIn InMail to connect with them and offer assistance. For example, "Bob, I noticed you are following Reid Hoffman, founder of LinkedIn. I do, as well. I thought you would be interested in seeing the attached article featuring Mr. Hoffman. Let me know if I can assist you in any way."

Another underutilized capability of LinkedIn is microtargeting your message to a particular group. From time to time, one of my companies will have an announcement that would appeal primarily to CEOs. Other times it might be a message about an investment that would appeal to a CFO. I then sort my contacts by job title and send an email on LinkedIn to the group that would be most interested.

Next, if I am traveling anywhere, I will always take a look at my LinkedIn contacts by location to figure out if there is someone in the area to which I am traveling with whom I need to reconnect.

Finally, realize that companies spend billions of dollars annually to drive their brand awareness. LinkedIn gives you an almost free ability to build your own brand and drive top-of-mind awareness. The beautiful thing is this: You are in control; you can build and define your own image in any way you would like. The net result is that it will enable you to link up more effectively as you grow your professional network.

Facebook

My second favorite place to link up online professionally is Facebook. That may surprise some, but as a result of business contacts I have made on Facebook, I have hired everything from an executive assistant to a chief financial officer. The shear enormity of people on Facebook together with the personalized nature of the information you find there makes it an important venue. Think about it: Roughly a quarter of the adult population of this planet has a Facebook profile. I am also of the philosophy that everything about relationships is personal—even in business. Facebook is the definitive place to learn more about potential business partners, customers, and clients on a personal level. I use Facebook to:

- Comment to others to show concern or interest. I don't just "like" something—I make a comment. It's more personal.
- Build social relationships.
- Privately or publicly post background, interests, and aspirations.
- Communicate directly by sending private messages using the Facebook platform. When I send a personalized message as opposed to just a like or a comment, my chances of a deeper connection increase.

- Categorize my Facebook friends by groups I designate.
- Post materials that will allow others to see you as a domain expert. My advice: Don't get too personal, political, or graphic, as your Facebook page will get viewed by future employers.
- Post positive quotes and messages.

Personal Email

Your personal email can be a beautiful tool to drive business results and link you up. Whenever I return from an event where I have collected business cards, I use a tool to read those cards and insert all contact information into my email contact list. As mentioned earlier, it is important when you add people to insert them into one or more groups or categories before closing out this process. It is interesting to note that each of the major email providers allows you to categorize a contact. There is a reason that functionality is there. Use it to ensure you remain linked up in useable ways with your connections.

In terms of remaining top of mind, I will send out blasts once a month or so to my entire email database. Note that Gmail has a daily limit of 500 emails, and Yahoo has one of 200. If you have thousands of contacts, you will need to use some form of contact management software from folks like Eloqua, MailChimp, or InfusionSoft to send out bulk communications.

Other Platforms

In terms of other social platforms, I am a reasonably active Twitter user, although due to the nature of that platform, I have not used it as robustly as some for linking up on a deeper level. Twitter does allow you to monitor real-time happenings and stay current on topics of interest to you. It further allows you to stay linked to experts in your field and "retweet" what they have written. I enjoy it when I am notified that a comment or quotation I have shared on Twitter has been reweeted broadly. It tells me that the person that has repurposed my thought is appreciative of my insight. Your goal of Twitter should be to have more "followers" than people you follow. Finally, Twitter is an important platform by which you can establish your reputation as an expert in your field.

Other social platforms that I use on occasion include Pinterest (80 million users), Instagram (140 million users), and Google+ (200 million plus and growing rapidly.) With Google behind Circles, it is becoming an increasingly important platform. I believe it will eventually give LinkedIn a run for its money. It also provides users with a number of preset groups into which you can place your contacts. Also, when I am in Gmail, if I hover over a connection, a simple icon pops up telling me into which groups I have placed a particular contact. It allows its users, very easily I might add, to remain linked up to hundreds of connections based on how you think of them in real life, such as "family," "friends," "business contacts," etc.

Let me add that with all of these twenty-first century tools of communication, you should *and can* always be networking. As emphasized earlier in this book, the best networkers I know are those who realize that networking is a life skill, not just something you decide to do when you need something from someone. In order to succeed at building your network, it is important to show up at events, link up with people in meaningful ways, follow up, and keep in touch. Leaders and other winning business professionals are exceptional at staying linked to others who might be great contacts today, tomorrow, or down the road.

Transform "Likes" into Relationships

The greatest key to harnessing the power of your networks is to move beyond agenda and tactic into genuine concern and service. Relationships are the goal; technology is simply the method. Confuse the two, and your impact will be wasted.

At the inception of the program we now call "Facebook" was the idea that people could participate and give input on pictures and topics. Originally, students were given two photo images and asked to determine the one they preferred. Now, Facebook has grown to be the number one pastime among those over 13 years old. Today there are over 1 billion Facebook users.

While the familiar email format of Yahoo, Gmail, etc. was a one-way street, Facebook created an open discussion, connecting people instantly through conversation. This changed the dynamics of the conversation from that of a tennis match to that of a basketball game; it was no longer a slow volley but a fast-paced hustle between many people on the court at once. Connections could happen instantly and be responded to within seconds by those reading the digital billboard. The concept of "forum" has revolutionized not only how individuals connect, but also how help is facilitated during global tragedies. Even citizens in socialized countries receive news and create uprisings using this tool.

Creator of Facebook, Mark Zuckerberg, acknowledged the global impact of that platform when he said: "By giving people the power to share, we're making the world more transparent."

The impact of the masses devouring insights *from* the masses, *by* the masses, is as great a revolution in information management as the Internet itself or the printing press. My belief is that from this growth, both the product innovation and the explosion of support and adoption into the mainstream *grow out of our innate need and thirst to be known and appreciated on a personal level.* All of the social media forums mentioned here feed that need.

The goal therefore in your connections with people is to genuinely move from a painless, random Facebook "like" to a long-term, mutually supportive business and personal interaction. Only here will relationships create engagement, commitment, and productivity with "win-win" outcomes.

Thousands of individuals have impacted my journey through email correspondence, LinkedIn messages, and Facebook posts. The trite saying, "One's career is always built on the shoulders of others" is absolutely true in my case. My interest, care, and concern for others' well-being have been mirrored in their reciprocal support. Time after time the doors that have opened in my career have been *through deep-rooted relationships*, not random "likes" or feigned flattery with a hopeful sale in the foreseeable future.

Seth Godin writes, "How can you squander even one more day not taking advantage of the greatest shifts of our generation? How dare you settle for less when the world has made it so easy for you to be remarkable?"

As you connect with others on Google+, LinkedIn, Twitter, and Facebook, ask yourself how your influence helps them. How do you support others? Do you genuinely connect in an effort to acknowledge others in their triumphs, their challenges, and their relationships? To what degree can you be transparent and let others see who you really are so they connect to you emotionally?

Study Your Networks

How do you connect emotionally to strangers on various forms of social media in a way that is effective and personable? Is it possible? My answer is "yes." Not only is it possible to do it that way, but to really Up Your Game it is essential. Let me teach you a way to grow your online network and presence. Take some time and go online. Study the networks of your best-connected and most successful friends. See who they are linked to and how. See what those connections look like and how they interact, present themselves online, and encourage each other. There is a lot that can be learned here.

I can give you an example of a relationship in my own life that came about through connecting genuinely online. When I was building my network on Facebook, one of my early friends was Dan Burton. Dan worked for me at Novell and led our government relations effort. Dan is known for his integrity and high quality of work in Washington D.C., so I trust Dan intuitively. I know that, in general terms, the people with whom he is connected are quality people. In business, for the most part, like attracts like. Remember this, and it will help you as you connect, as well.

Dan now works for SalesForce.com as a Senior VP of Government Relations. Salesforce is lucky to have such a great employee. As I was perusing his database of Facebook friends, I noticed that he was directly connected to Marc Benioff, founder and CEO of Salesforce.com. I thought to myself, "Now that is someone with whom I would like to be connected. He has built a terrific company, and there is much I can learn from a man like that." At the time, I had just become CEO of Fusion-io and hoped the connection might serve us both. I reached out to Mark.

However, I did not simply send him an open invitation to join me on Facebook. Generic invites are pretty weak. It would have looked like, "David Bradford wants to be your friend on Facebook." When I receive an invitation like that, especially when I don't know the person, I am not nearly as receptive as when it is more personalized. Knowing that Marc and I might be similar that way, I created a carefully worded, personalized invitation for Marc to be my friend on Facebook.

Dear Marc:

We have a mutual friend in Dan Burton, your head of Government Relations at Salesforce. Congratulations on your many successes there. Dan worked for me when I was an Exec at Novell. I recently became CEO of a fast-growing technology company, "Fusion-io." I was even able to get the inventor of the Apple computer, Steve Wozniak, to come work with us. I thought I would reach out on Facebook and invite you to be my friend.

Best regards, David

He responded positively, and we made the connection. I also connected with his Senior VP of Human Resources, Erin Flynn, in a similar way. That connection turned into a series of very positive meetings between HireVue and SalesForce.com culminating in Salesforce becoming a HireVue customer.

I saw a sign at my gym the other day. It read, "Commitment is a muscle." I thought about that and realized that the more you stick to something, just like working a muscle, the stronger it gets. It is important to recognize *the multiplier effect of networking.* The more people you have, the greater the power and efficacy of your network. Stay connected. Stay committed to adding people to your network. I do this every day. When you add one person, the value of your network increases by more than just one—it increases exponentially because of the connections that person brings.

Connect Authentically

I once read that within the physical body are receptors. Our eyes, our fingertips, our ears, our senses of taste and smell, and even our intuitive minds receive information that is then filtered in our brains prior to making a decision. This is significant to understand about the impressions you project through technology and social media. Just like taking an invisible polygraph test, your audience is asking questions about you, your message, your brand, and your sincerity. There is no way to shortcut this process or fool it. The only way to leverage it is to work on your own sincerity. Do you genuinely care about others, or is your caring limited to their purchasing of something you offer? Do you want the best for people outside of your own agenda for them?

Personalize Your Connections

Personalize the way you interact, share information and resources, and offer support and encouragement. One of the keys to successful communications in any social media is to be sincere, unique, and approachable. There is an old adage referred to earlier in this book that tells us that people "don't care how much you know until they know how much you care."

Every day I probably spend an hour on LinkedIn and Facebook connecting with our key customers as well as with key customer prospects. In just the last 24 hours, I sent messages on LinkedIn to roughly five different customers or prospects. But note: Each time I do this, I make it a *personalized* message. I study their profiles online—their education, their activities, and their business experience—and make it a point to comment positively on their backgrounds. As you personalize your connections, note things that are significant to your contact, like his college mascot or his enjoyment of golf, tennis, science, or whatever it might be. You may see from her Facebook profile things that stand out that create a common interest or speaking point. Build from this information and allow it to open conversations that lead to ideal outcomes.

The "Ideal" Experience: Connect Emotionally

People want ideal outcomes. They hope for quality customer service, genuine listening, and the ability to problem solve by the companies that serve them. While you may not have had those thoughts in regard to your personal brand on Facebook, Twitter, and LinkedIn, the same expectations apply. Give your network a better experience of you and the type of resource you can be to them, and they will trust you with their resources, as well.

Are your brand, your character, your product, and your communication with your network giving them permission to be better, kinder, or more gracious? Are you compelling them to be better, to think higher, and to connect more in their lives and in their businesses? Do you personally model this? Through your example, are you moving your customers and your network through the initial first impression and into real engagement?

Within every profile on Facebook, LinkedIn, and Twitter is the desire for a Happily Ever After. People are searching in the best way they know how to live their dreams and create a better reality for themselves. Understanding this, you can position yourself to be a resource and an influence using your marketing, your character, and your impact to buoy them up and inspire them to greatness. When you do this, you can create a ripple of impact that goes farther than a simple email or Facebook post. Use your words to fuel and encourage those within your cyber-reach. People will remember your positive impact and influence.

All business is personal. Get others to connect on an emotional level, and it will compel them to action. Connect with your audience and your network in a way that affirms their spirit, and it will compel them to even greater action.

Measure Success in Terms of Impact

All of our life successes are defined within the context of their impact on people—ourselves first, then impact on family, community, and world. Without people, on a small scale or large, no innovation in technology would be of significant value. Without people, our lives lack depth, connection, and passion.

Two of the most talented people I have ever interacted with are Bill Gates and Gary Kildall. Gary Kildall and Bill Gates have had arguably the most profound impact on the history of personal computing of any two people except possibly Steve Jobs and Steve Wozniak. They defined the age of personal computing, and their contributions continue to have a major impact on business in the twenty-first century. Why do people easily recognize the name of Bill Gates but not the name of Gary Kildall? What is the marked difference in the notoriety of these two people? The answer to these questions give us key insights about networking and building relationships.

When you go back today to your laptop, PDA, or personal computer network after finishing this chapter of the book, I want you to remember Gary Kildall and Bill Gates and try to learn from their experiences. Naturally, it will be a lot easier to remember Mr. Gates. But let me be clear, you would not be computing or communicating in the way you do today but for the life and business contributions of Gary Kildall.

In 1991, in my role as Head of Business Development and General Counsel of Novell, I was in the middle of Novell's acquisition of Gary Kildall's company. Before Gary died tragically in a bar fight in Monterey, California, in 1994, I interacted with Gary substantially and helped file the first antitrust complaint against Microsoft in 1992.

Kildall's career spans the history of the personal computer, which he was instrumental in popularizing in the 1970s. It has been said that Gary Kildall's technical contributions in the beginning days of microcomputing were valuable beyond anyone else's. His innovations included both the technical development of the personal computer operating system and the deployment of an equitable, consumer-oriented pricing model that is still in use today.

In 1972, Kildall was an associate professor of computer science at the U.S. Naval Postgraduate School in Monterey, California, and a consultant for Intel Corp., which had created the world's first microprocessor chip the year before. Kildall wrote a version of a computer programming language that worked on the chip, the Intel 4004. A year later, frustrated with the difficulty of making the 4004 work with disk drives and other computer components, he wrote the first personal computer operating system.

The operating program, called "Control Program for Micro-Computers" and shortened to "CP/M," offered hobbyists a way to use their microcomputers, as they were then called, in the same way as larger minicomputers and mainframes. Before this time, computers were programmed in painful and time-consuming ways by, for example, flipping switches on the front panel of the machines. There was no keyboard from which data could be input into the device. With CP/M, a person could type instructions on a keyboard, store data, and view results on a screen or printer.

CP/M soon became the standard operating system for personal computers. By 1981, Kildall was one of the best-known figures in a burgeoning multibillion-dollar personal computer business, and his $10 million company had sold over a quarter of a million versions of CP/M.

What about Bill Gates? Was he the father of the personal computer? No, not by any stretch. Did he invent DOS? No. Did he invent Windows? No. And he arguably has not created a new technology since he dropped out of Harvard in the mid 1970's. Nevertheless, he has created what was the world's most valuable company, and he is one of the world's richest men and the biggest charitable giver in history.

Why is Bill Gates one of the richest men on planet Earth and Gary Kildall a forgotten footnote in the annals of the computer industry? The fundamental reason is that Gates and Microsoft were about developing relationships that enabled them to secure an agreement to supply the desktop Operating System for the IBM Personal Computer. Kildall did not secure that agreement. Why? What factor prevented the inventor of the PC Operating System from securing the most important contract in the history of the computer industry?

Arguably, it can be boiled down to the fact that Gates understood *the power of personal relationships in business* and Kildall did not care about them. Certainly, there were many details involved, but I can cite at least two key factors of great impact.

1. Kildall admittedly disliked business. In a 1981 interview, Kildall said that he engaged in business just because he hoped "to support my computer habits" with the proceeds. He also disdained engaging with others in business in any type of meaningful way. In fact, on the day IBM came to Monterey, California, to negotiate "the contract of the century," Kildall was out flying in his airplane. He later explained to me that he thought IBM had shown up "too early" for the meeting. Truth be told, in those days, if IBM were flying into town, it would be seen as a pivotal meeting. Bottom line: Personal relationships did not seem like a priority to Gary.

2. Bill Gates developed personal relationships in business and was ready when IBM came calling. One of those relationships was with a gentleman by the name of Tim Paterson, President of Seattle Computing Products. After IBM's failed attempts to get a deal done with Gary Kildall, IBM contacted Bill Gates. Bill was clever and resourceful and knew the value of his computer industry colleagues. He built synergistic alliances that opened doors to the resources he needed. He did not have a PC operating system himself, but he knew someone who did. He acquired his PC operating system version for $50,000 from a tiny company called Seattle Computing Products. The operating system, Q-DOS (which stood for "Quick and Dirty Operating System"), had been designed by the company's programmer, Tim Paterson, who soon went to work for Microsoft. They renamed the product MS-DOS for Microsoft Disk Operating System, and Mr. Gates went back to IBM to get a deal done.

In a contractual masterstroke, Microsoft was allowed to license MS-DOS to IBM. Under the terms of the contract, Gates preserved for Microsoft the rights to license this new OS to other manufacturers, spawning an industry of "IBM-compatible" personal computers that depended upon Microsoft's operating system.

Bill Gates positioned himself through establishing key business relationships. This was the defining variable that made the difference in the careers of these two powerful men. Kildall became known as the guy who blew the deal of the century. Bill Gates became known as one of the most successful men in the world.

Invest Time and Purpose in People

Building your network in a powerful, effective way has everything to do with genuine investment of time and purpose in people. People connect to sincerity and disconnect if they sense you aren't really interested in them. People desire positive outcomes, inspiring connections, and affirming experiences. They want to feel better, do better, and have better results in their lives.

As Albert Schweitzer said, "In everyone's life, at some time, our inner fire goes out. It is then burst into flame by an encounter with another human being. We should all be thankful for those people who rekindle the inner spirit." By being curious, building win-win relationships, connecting on multiple platforms, studying our relationships, and connecting authentically, we can have the power to light a fire within someone and make an impact in meaningful ways.

Are we building up others and linking up in meaningful ways to ensure actionable relationships? Are you linking up to Up Your Game on a daily basis?

CHAPTER 6 GAME PLAN

1. In order to begin linking up with others online, start with your wedding list. Invite them all to connect with you on LinkedIn, Twitter, Instagram, or Facebook. The average person has roughly 250 people they can invite to a wedding.

2. It has been said that you are the average of the five people you surround yourself with, so be sure to link up with top-notch people and make those interactions personal ones.

3. Remember that you can learn something from everyone. Never underestimate the impact that a single individual can have on your life and business.

4. Reach out on occasion to someone you may not have met previously using LinkedIn, Facebook, or Twitter. But when requesting that another link up with you on social media, send a personal note and not just the generic: "I would like to add you to my professional network on LinkedIn."

5. When using social media, don't tell people what you are eating for dinner. Tell them something that might change their life. Make it personal.

6. Get to know people above you and below you. Think of the world as more flat in terms of relationships, not so hierarchically.

PRINCIPLE 5: STAND UP

Reputations, simply put, are the beliefs and opinions that are generally held about someone. Think to yourself: Would you ever do business with someone that you know has a bad reputation? The obvious answer is "no." So my advice to all, as simple as it may seem, is this: Never engage in any activity in your personal or professional life online or offline that would cause someone to question your honor or character. Instead, be a stand-up person, one with whom people have a genuine desire to do business. Stand up for what is right, and people will honor and respect your beliefs. They will also turn to you as a leader. By standing up throughout your career, you will be upping your game and experience success.

The importance of maintaining a sterling character is magnified in today's world of social media. One billion people use Google search every day. More than one billion are Facebookers, and 300 million people are using LinkedIn. In contrast, at the height of the network television domination by CBS, ABC, and NBC in the late 70's, only 35 million people watched TV every day. I cannot overstate the importance of how you look to the billions that may be watching you! Your online reputation is of critical importance. You must be seen as a stand-up person and one who honors relationships.

About 100 years ago, the founder of Brigham Young University was asked to describe what he meant by the word "honor." Karl G. Maeser replied: "I will tell you. Place me behind prison walls—walls of stone ever so high, ever so thick, reaching ever so far into the ground—there is a possibility that in some way or another I may escape; but stand me on the floor and draw a chalk line around me and have me give my word of honor never to cross it. Can I get out of the circle? No. Never! I'd die first!"

Being someone of unshakeable character provides a key foundation for your credibility. There are two things you must know about credibility to be a stand-up success: Credibility must be earned, and credibility must be kept. To use your credibility to your advantage, surround yourself with credibility, build your credibility on social media, associate with others who have credibility, and invest in your own PR. When it comes to building credibility on social media, be selective in the connections you make, categorize, and personalize. You'll be building high-quality, interesting, and mutually satisfying connections in no time.

You can do everything else I recommend in this book—show up, follow up, give without getting—but no one will be willing to do business with you if you are not a stand-up person. Your credibility in business and in life is priceless and a necessary element to utilizing your network effectively.

Another reason to be a stand-up person is the invasive evolution of social media and the Internet. Those who grasp the significance of building an honorable reputation and who develop the character to maintain it will succeed. Those who don't, won't. Social media only enhances one's reputation . . . for good or for bad. Stated another way, the Internet and social media *make you more of what you already are.*

Credibility Is Earned

It's not enough to have a sleek business card and a handful of claims about your business prowess. LinkedIn and Facebook now make it easy for curious parties to research a person or company's track record, and a quick Google search can pull up scientific evidence and qualified specialists. The average American teenager has the technical know-how to debunk the hype of an unproven leader or product in the market in seconds.

Today's success goes to those whose personal brands and products can weather the test of time and stand strong under scrutiny from a much savvier buyer than ever before. Long forgotten is the peddler selling snake oil to backwards townspeople. The customer is king, because he or she has access to more information than in marketplaces of the past. Products and services with strong reputations gain momentum, while shady businesses and individuals fall to a very public death.

Unfortunately, we see this often with highly paid athletes, political hopefuls, and big-screen celebrities. Scandalous or irresponsible choices in the moment can make their way to the national headlines in hours. Health code violations or poor employee treatment can destroy a product or a national company in a millisecond, when it may have taken decades to build. A bright political hopeful may have skeletons long silenced come to life in a pivotal race, ending a career of high aspirations and hard work. Again, credibility must be earned, and it must be maintained.

One example of personal integrity that was earned in a powerful way is a story involving Jon M. Huntsman, Sr., the founder of the Huntsman Chemical companies, which became one of the largest private corporations in the world. I knew John Sr. a bit from my work with Jon Jr. when the latter was elected Governor of Utah, and I served as general counsel for his transition team.

As the story goes, in the early years of founding the Huntsman empire, it was necessary for his company to sell part of the business. Jon Huntsman agreed to sell a certain percentage of the company for $53 million. The parties involved in the transaction shook hands on the deal and then proceeded with the arduous task of due diligence, which would lead to a closure of the transaction. There was a lot of delay in the process of bringing the two entities together, and the process became attenuated. During this time, Jon's company was exploding with new growth. Finally, the day came to close the transaction and finalize the deal. Due to the outstanding growth of Jon's company, the deal, on paper, turned out to be worth more like $250 million to the buyer rather than the $53 million agreed upon. Jon Huntsman had a legal right to rearrange the terms of their agreement and seek more money for the company he was selling. Instead, he said something to the following effect: "I shook your hand. I made an agreement. The price will be $53 million. That's what we agreed to six months ago." Talk about earning credibility! This is what great leaders do. If you want to be known as a stand-up person, make sure your word is your bond.

In today's world, your reputation can be lost in nanoseconds. As I read in Forbes recently, "At no point in history has it been this easy to destroy your entire life so quickly." Remember Anthony Weiner, the promising New York congressman who was ousted after sending sexual pictures of himself to a number of women? How about Kenneth Cole, the noted fashion designer who personally tweeted the following tasteless verbiage when millions were rioting in Egypt: "Millions are in uproar in #Cairo. Rumor is they heard our new spring collection is available online." Or think about the saga of InterActiveCorp PR executive

Justine Sacco, who had her reputation largely destroyed when she tweeted a racist comment before boarding a long flight. By the time she landed, essentially the whole world knew.

The lesson is that your tweets, your posts, and your shares may all be seen by millions. If you are striving to be a leader in your particular field or industry, assume that all of your posts are matters of public record. If you want to accelerate your move to the top, don't let anything you have shared in social media circles create a blot on what people may think of you down the road. When I have a post or comment that I suspect may be controversial or inappropriate in any way, I stop and wait at least 24 hours before sharing it publicly.

To reinforce this point, I recall evaluating a particular person for a specific role in HireVue. I went to her Facebook page and LinkedIn profile. The LinkedIn profile looked great, but there were some inappropriate photos on Facebook. This immediately caused me to rethink this person's fit for a job at our company. I simply told my Human Resources team to write to this individual and let her know that, while we appreciated her interest in the position, we had found a better candidate.

As a senior executive, I want people on my team that I can trust will represent our company in the best possible way—both on the job and off. If trusted resources recommend you as a businessperson, this is a big deal for me. Every employer wants this, as does every person creating strategic alliances, building business partnerships, or planning an event or large venture. If you can win credibility with people in positions of influence, doors will open to you. This requires you to be consistent, honest, honorable, and cooperative—and do this for long periods of time. In many ways, the pendulum is swinging back to giving your word, working hard, having integrity, and being committed. Sadly, for too long, many have thought these virtues passé.

Brit Hume once said, "In the end, you make your reputation and you have your success based upon credibility and being able to provide people who are really hungry the information they want." How does credibility, or lack of it, impact your reputation? What builds your credibility? What destroys or undermines it? How do credibility issues make or break your career in ways so important that you find yourself difficult to employ? And what miniscule changes should you make today that will increase your career possibilities a hundredfold in the next ten years? To be successful in building and maintaining credibility, you must keep your credibility, use it to your advantage, surround yourself with stand-up people, stand up for what is right, stand with other successful professionals, invest in your own brand, build social media credibility, and test your connections.

Credibility Must Be Kept

As a busy professional, I simply cannot spend the time on individuals that come with average to poor recommendations; conversely, if someone comes emphatically endorsed by someone I trust, his or her credibility and my interest in hiring him or her increases exponentially. *Credibility is the litmus test.* If you have gained credibility with someone I trust, then I almost automatically have trust for you. If you receive a metaphorical gold star from one of my resources, I assume you have some serious talent.

I have been blessed in my career to keep company with some of the best and brightest minds of our time, from Eric Schmidt, chairman and former CEO of Google, to Larry Sonsini, the preeminent securities lawyer in America, to Presidential candidate Mitt Romney, to key individuals in the venture capital world and beyond. These associations have pushed me to do better, learn more, and lead wisely. Of critical importance is the ability to have their support, loyalty, and referrals when needed.

A thumbs-up from someone smart, reliable, and skilled in the industry, like the people mentioned above, allows me to cut through the riff-raff and take action immediately. One positive referral such as this saves me approximately five hours researching the backgrounds of a handful of candidates. If I were to randomly hire someone and the person was the wrong fit, the cost could be enormous. Large companies can spend upwards of $100,000 training a new employee, paying wages, covering health plans, and putting stock options in place, all to lose that money if the person cannot perform in his or her position. This is where credibility plays into business decisions and where social media can positively or negatively shine a light on you as an individual seeking success. A passive presence in these arenas can undermine your credibility, whereas a purposeful profile can enhance the lighting on your best professional features.

Remember, too, that the Web has given companies unprecedented access to potential job candidates and their online personas. The competition for talent is tough. If there is any appreciable negativity to your online profile, you are toast.

Have you won the respect of honorable, measured leaders in your professional and personal life? Do you know reputable people who would vouch for your name, your job performance, and your morals? A positive answer to these questions will absolutely make the difference in your income and your upward mobility in your industry—and quite possibly save your hide if you end up in deep water or circumstances that require more knowledge and insight than what you have on your own.

I encourage you to do a personal inventory and assess how effective you are at gaining and maintaining credibility with key influential people and using social media tools to portray that personally and professionally. Be sure to study your online profile—know yourself and how you are being perceived online.

Are you standing out and standing up? And never, ever post anything that would cause someone to question your integrity or commitment.

How to Use Credibility to Your Advantage

When I was announced as HireVue's new CEO, a couple of my good industry friends, Steve Wozniak and Eric Schmidt, offered public endorsements in the press release. That was a major help in establishing credibility for HireVue. I am grateful that those friends would be kind enough to show up for me when asked. It is a tribute to their fundamental graciousness and also a testament to the powerful principle of standing up—by surrounding yourself with credibility. Your goal to Up Your Game and make it to the top must include associating yourself with successful professionals and investing in your own brand to ensure it remains unsullied.

Surround Yourself with Stand-Up People

Early in my career as CEO at Fusion-io, I struggled. I was concerned about the company, my position, and our ability to take the right course of action in many areas. The strategy for growth was unclear, and there were many possibilities presenting themselves. My leadership in the company required me to make big decisions that would impact the business, its employees, and the product long term. It was daunting. During the same time, parallel to what I was experiencing personally and professionally, a good friend of mine, Stephen M.R. Covey, wrote and published a book called *The Speed of Trust*. He distinguished himself as a great business mind with his concepts. I was able to call him directly, read the book, and ask him for specific advice. He taught me great lessons about the importance of trust and how significant that is in laying the foundation for a solid company. The sales guy must trust the marketing guy, who must have the support and trust of the engineering VP, who must trust his chief financial officer, and so on. We were missing some management pieces in the organization at the time and lacked the components of trust that Stephen Covey spoke to me about.

I followed Stephen's advice and sought to fill those seats with great people that had wonderful reputations and track records. I was in a new position with very real concerns, and connecting with Stephen assisted me greatly in the level of success we were able to achieve. He taught me a great deal about teams. When trust exists in an organization, everything accelerates. When trust doesn't exist, things slow down because people will always be trying, from the CEO down, to cover their own tracks. This nervousness breeds problems—when trust is lacking, people are afraid to take bold action.

I was so impressed with Covey's concept that I extended an invitation for him to join the advisory board for Fusion-io. I had seen firsthand the value of his leadership skills, and he also trusted my business sense and background enough to help us succeed. I didn't need to call on him regularly—but when I did call, I received the best possible advice because of his world-class knowledge of corporate organization and ability to drive trust and communication within a company.

So, my advice to you is to build a network of people around you who have skills and talents to advise and counsel you. By the same token, you must also support, encourage, and invest in their success.

Stand Up for What Is Right on Facebook, LinkedIn, and Twitter

Today, the great litmus test for credibility is the Internet. With a simple Google search, anyone can learn your address and phone number. With an equally simple search on Facebook, LinkedIn, and Twitter, a stranger can deduce much about your personality, your hobbies, and your relationships. Ask yourself this question: What would a stranger surmise about your character by browsing your LinkedIn profile, your Twitter feeds, or your Facebook page? Recruiters will search your social postings before hiring you. What will they discover?

People make judgments about the information they are given. If your Facebook page is filled with negativity, a recruiter will assume this is your personality. If your LinkedIn profile is missing positive testimonials of your work, then it will lead a prospective employer to a conclusion. If your associations lack credibility or professionalism, it may be assumed that you do also. This may or may not be an accurate assessment of you as a person; however, people on the outside looking in only have the information placed before them with which to make decisions.

In an interview discussing today's technologies and how they impact the bottom line of professional credibility, founder of LinkedIn Reid Hoffman stated, "Once how you treat people, how you work, and how you live becomes part of your network image, then all of a sudden people have an incentive to be good . . . because you live with it for years and decades to come." Today's online accessibility to people's professional history and reputation through Google search, Klout, and LinkedIn gives new transparency to those researching an individual for a job or affiliation. Take this seriously and build your profiles, your resumes, and your network in a way that promotes growth and success. Step by credible step, you will see the rewards multiply.

Stand Up with Other Successful Professionals

As you seek to grow your credibility online through the platforms of Facebook, LinkedIn, Google+, and Twitter, a powerful tool you have is your association with other people. You may not realize it, but *those with whom you connect online either add to your credibility or undermine it.* They are seen as a reflection of your interests, your values, and your business. Choose your associations wisely, and take the time to assess whether they promote the things you believe.

While many people see Facebook and LinkedIn as a place to grow mass popularity, measured and specific growth is the best method for one's career and reputation. Adding random names and numbers to your contact base does not necessarily equate to good growth, and wrong connections can undermine your desired impact. One way to build your credibility is to increase your online associations with those who project professionalism and success. Accept invitations with discernment, and extend invitations to those who are qualified in their fields. As you sift through invitations, assess and categorize your contacts. This serves you in two ways: first, you have now qualified them as a positive connection, and second, you have now placed them in a category which allows you to "pool" your resources for future needs.

I receive multiple daily LinkedIn requests to connect with people. Probably 75 percent are from people I have never met. Some people automatically reject requests from unknown individuals, but I am of the philosophy that you never know who might be your next great, important connection. Nearly everyone has something to offer. So before just automatically rejecting them, I look at two things: Who are our mutual connections? And who has endorsed this person? With respect to point #1, I believe that, in business, like attracts like. If this person is affiliated with a number of successful people, then my interest level increases.

I then go one step further. I look at this person's endorsements and recommendations. If this person has been positively recommended on LinkedIn by folks I know and trust, then I will likely add him or her. Written recommendations are more important to me than simple endorsements. LinkedIn has a feature called "endorsements" on its site. It is a capability that allows anyone to endorse another for specific skills. These are different than specific recommendations that are written. Some have called this new endorsement capability "Recommendations Light." Like it or not, people will look at those endorsements—particularly those who might think of hiring you or partnering with you.

Facebook has its own method for helping you qualify and quantify those with whom you surround yourself. Building connections with solid individuals can add credibility, add wisdom, and add vision to your personal and professional world. Purposefully choosing how and when to align with people can shorten your learning curve, open doors, and help you avoid devastating mistakes. Start now to choose wisely those with whom you associate and trust—both online and offline.

If you have the option to add or "friend" people, and they do not look reputable or their pictures on Facebook are less than noble, opt out. It is not helpful to your personal or professional credibility to add contacts that tarnish your reputation or position you to appear connected to shady characters. Distance yourself in a polite way from those things that would have you grouped with individuals who are not credible or trustworthy. Be mindful that your photographs also give others a private tour into your values, your "likes" and your character. Are there things on your Facebook wall or timeline that detract from your character? Are there photographs that harm your credibility or reputation by adding a dimension of immorality, or are of a provocative nature, that may influence potential business associates or professional strategic alliances?

Most companies know it is a liability to employ individuals that project less than trustworthy personas. These companies and leaders do their homework and scrutinize that background and presentation of potential employee candidates. To raise the bar in your personal and professional life, you may need to do some housecleaning and remove anything that detracts from your own credibility. This could include wall posts, comments on others' walls, improper photographs, and even questionable social events you may have attended. Your credibility is at stake.

Invest in Your Own Brand

Many CEOs hire out their social media postings. They have an office staffer post comments or smart quotes to their wall. I take the opposite tactic. No one can represent my persona and credibility in the way I can. I purposely choose to make my own comments, tweet my own tweets, and add likes and endorsements where they apply. Doing this commenting and screening myself allows me the opportunity to meet the individuals and determine how we connect, how I see us working together, and if I believe it can be a win-win connection. Paying an employee to do this may save me time. However, that staff person cannot be me in the relationship, *and it is the relationship that makes the magic happen.*

Protect your reputation and your honor. Protect your credibility in the eyes of others so that you can easily and confidently connect with others and create mutually supportive relationships. While this requires vigilance and wisdom, the rewards of having social credibility online far outweigh the investment of personal effort and time.

Building Social Media Credibility

So, what makes people credible in the world of social media? Of course, it helps to have a large number of connections, friends and followers—but that's just a start. People who build and maintain credibility in the digital world have numerous high-quality relationships with respected people . . . who respect them. When it comes to building credibility on social media, be selective in the connections you make, categorize, and personalize. You'll soon have a respectable network.

Three Tests to Select Connections

There are three tests that I use to screen potential connections on Facebook, LinkedIn, Google+, Foursquare, Instagram, and Pinterest. Each test, or area of screening, gives me a different angle to discern more information about the person presenting his or her profile. For simplicity's sake, I'll focus on Facebook in the paragraphs that follow.

Test #1: Look at your potential connection's friends and followers. Facebook allows you to have 5,000 friends. I have maxed out and currently have 256 friend requests pending. To me, it is important that I choose my friends personally. I want to be engaged in the process and truly get to know these people so we can help each other. So I want to see the people who link us to each other.

As I browse over the names of our mutual friends, if I see people that I respect, the potential of my accepting the friend request increases. I also look at the person's pictures. Photos alone do not create credibility, but they can quickly disqualify someone.

I also look to see how many people follow a given individual. This gives me a sense of how much they are looked at in their area of specialty or in the community in general. Do people care what he/she posts? Are the posts interesting? Do they motivate people? Do they inspire others?

Test #2: Look at the "likes." This gives me insight into what he or she finds interesting. If someone chooses not to list much about his or her business experience or background and gives only basic information, then I will message him or her personally and say, "Thank you for reaching out to me via Facebook. Can you tell me more about your background and interests?" In many ways, what I am saying is, "Help me get to know you better so I can make a conscientious decision on whether or not to add you."

Test #3: Check out the photos and videos. With social media painting a bigger picture of an individual, new arenas are being impacted. A friend of mine participates in a statewide beauty pageant program with a panel of judges. Similar to a job interview situation, judges now have access to pageant contestant names and locations. This makes it easy for searches to be done on each contestant, giving a snapshot of the credibility or lack of credibility of those vying for the title. Web pages, blogs, and You-Tube videos can be found to support or negate the volunteer efforts and interests, as well as the reputation, professionalism, and depth of the contestant's message. In some cases, inappropriate material and posts influence a judge's scoring and undermine a contestant's best efforts. The same can be true when a job candidate projects an image online that is offensive or not in harmony with a specific company or industry. Are there photos or videos posted on Facebook that detract from her professionalism? Does she present herself in a manner congruent to her title or position? Much can and will be assumed by what is posted on social media.

Conclusion

Being credible is all related to how you come across to others. Are you consistently interested? Are you consistently helpful? Are you interested in and concerned about what people need next in their personal lives or business to be more successful? Do you follow through on your words with trustworthy action? If you do, you can expect to create a team of mutually supportive, categorized, effective friendships and partnerships around you. With this type of synergy and support, you can exponentially Up Your Game and increase your outcomes in life and business.

Professional sports teams have the same experience. They operate as large networks. Where there is great fan support, the teams tend to up their own games. An example of this is the

Boston Red Sox or the New York Yankees who sell out night after night after night—and they are at the top of their division year after year. Let's look at a contrast between two baseball teams and how this support makes the synergetic difference on a large scale. The San Diego Padres are blessed with the best climate in the universe and a city that likes outdoor events. However, during the all-important 2010 Pennant chase when the Padres and the San Francisco Giants were going neck and neck, when you would think fan support would be at its highest, the Padres home games were poorly attended. In the stands, thousands of seats sat empty. In contrast, despite colder weather and tougher conditions, the San Francisco Giants sold out night after night and were the beneficiaries of great fan support. The Giants went on to win the pennant and eventually the World Series. They were able to Up Their Game on the field as a direct result of the enthusiastic backing of their fans.

We all need fan support. Just like a professional sports team, you have people who are rooting for you—people who want you to succeed in the business of life. By the same token, you have friends and business associates you enjoy working with—people you want to see succeed. Your ability to show up for them, be credible, network, support, and reciprocate on a daily basis can give you a competitive edge. Just like a professional athlete, you have a fan base of skilled people around you that want to help you win. To be credible, you must serve others by being a fan for them.

In the end, to Up Your Game, you will need to stand up. Have you developed sufficient credibility for people to take action on your behalf when asked?

CHAPTER 7 GAME PLAN

1. Never, ever do anything in your personal or business life online or offline that would cause people to question your integrity. Credibility means everything to your networking success.

2. Become a Domain Expert on a given topic. People will look to network with you because you have stood up for something and know a particular subject matter better than others.

3. When you make a promise to follow up, do it.

4. To communicate openly and effectively with others and form a basis of trust, remember to stick to your principles but abandon your assumptions.

5. Your future employers will look at your online profiles. The competition is tough. Make sure there are no negative or inappropriate aspects of your LinkedIn, Facebook, or Twitter profiles.

6. Your ability to incorporate the power of mass collaboration in solving business issues is directly proportional to the degree that you have helped others in the past and the degree that you are seen as someone with credibility.

PRINCIPLE 6: SCALE UP

The story is told of two woodcutters who decided to compete against one another to see which of them could cut down more trees in an eight-hour period of time. They started simultaneously; but, after one hour, one of them heard that the other had stopped cutting trees. The first woodcutter, believing that this was his opportunity to gain a competitive advantage, redoubled his efforts. Ten minutes passed, and he heard the second woodcutter recommence his endeavors. After about another hour, the first cutter heard that his combatant had stopped again. Feeling confident that he had gained an important edge in the competition, the first woodcutter continued to chop continuously.

This continued throughout the day with one woodcutter stopping for ten minutes and the other working nonstop. The first woodcutter was completely certain he had won the prize but was dismayed to learn that he finished a distant second to cutter number two. "How did it happen?" he asked his competitor. "Very simple," answered the second woodcutter. "Each hour, I stopped my work for ten minutes. When you were busy cutting trees, I sharpened my ax."

There is no doubt that both woodcutters worked very hard, but the second woodcutter secured his victory by working smart and efficiently.

Building a world-class network takes hard work, time, and and smart organization. With each passing day, one needs to do something to scale up his or her network to make it as efficient and usable as possible. To scale up your network effectively, you have to do two things: work hard and work smart. Interestingly, the same thing is true of becoming a great leader.

Vince Lombardi, the famous football coach, once said: "Leaders aren't born. They are made. And they are made just like anything else—through hard work. And that's the price we'll have to pay to achieve that goal, or any goal." And I might add that includes the goal of building a scaled-up, world-class network.

Working hard requires tenacity and discipline. Working smart requires analyzing a problem and finding the quickest, most effective strategy to solving it. In my years of business and leadership, I have seen that building a strong network is the smartest "hard work" you can do. It can open doors, align you with others with complementary skill sets, and place you in the presence of people who know things you do not know—thus shortening the learning curve in any endeavor or business pursuit. By leveraging your connections, prioritizing your relationships, working with the end in mind, making the law of reciprocity work for you, using social media, giving it all you've got, and building a killer team, you too can scale up and successfully Up Your Game and your chances for success.

Persist in Scaling Up Your Network

Networking is plain hard work. One must first create the connections, then organize, feed, cultivate, and nurture them with consistent, committed follow-up. Most importantly, one must perform these tasks even when momentum is low, drive has dwindled, and outlooks are not promising. Enthusiasm is often lost in the minutia, and profound impact does not happen instantaneously. Hype for the endeavor will not be enough to keep one committed to the required effort. This is why many will give up on the program and settle for less-than-stellar results. Building and maintaining a killer network requires real, hard work.

NFL Hall of Fame quarterback Steve Young once shared with me his experience in battling against his arch nemesis, the Green Bay Packers, in an important NFL playoff game. The morning of the big game, he awoke and looked outside. True to the weather forecast from the previous day, the skies had opened up and there was a massive rainstorm that had hit the area. His initial thoughts were about the muddy field, his inability to run effectively, the difficulty his small hands would have in gripping the ball, and how the wind might impact his passing. He was discouraged. However, at that point, Steve knelt down and engaged in an important moment of meditation. He got up and said to himself, "Some things in life you cannot get around; you have to go straight through." Steve made it through that game with a major victory—one that led him to many more and eventually to a Super Bowl win and induction into the Pro Football Hall of Fame.

If you want to be successful at any endeavor, there are days when you just have to push ahead despite the obstacles. Some days, it may be difficult to show up. Other days, you may not feel motivated to follow up. At other times, you may be tempted to not stand up. But winners and leaders move forward and build a world-class professional network.

When you network with others of differing skill sets, you can add their unique strengths to your tool belt. You multiply your strength a hundredfold. One person alone cannot run a company. Sharing the responsibility of a corporation by growing a synergistic team is the smartest way to work hard in leadership.

Years ago, as the new CEO of Fusion-io, one of my responsibilities was to recruit a new VP of Global Sales. Despite the turmoil surrounding Fusion-io when I arrived, the board still had high expectations for the company in terms of sales. Fusion-io was in the process of closing a Series B round of financing led by Lightspeed Ventures, the venture capital fund that was targeted to lead the round. Lightspeed Ventures had been promised certain performance outcomes. In order to retain their interest and ensure financing for the company, we had to perform. Although there had been major turmoil at the company, and although I had to let go half of the sales force, we were still expected to bring in considerable revenue. I had to move quickly.

About that time, I attended a conference in Santa Barbara. I was walking the beach and visiting with Scott Sandell, a managing partner at New Enterprise Associates (NEA), one of the top ten venture capital funds in the world, and another investor in Fusion-io. In reference to my concerns about Fusion-io and our need for new talent, Scott strongly suggested I retain a professional recruiting firm to help with the process. We both recognized the importance of bringing together a great management team to move the company forward. Scott's recommendation was a good one, and I valued his insight. Normally, I would be very acquiescent in a situation like that. After all, NEA was the first institutional investor in Fusion-io. They had entrusted me with millions of dollars in capital and, not unreasonably, expected results.

After Scott had given me the names of a couple of first-rate recruiting firms, I turned to him and said, "Scott, just give me a couple of months. I have developed quite a network of personal contacts in the IT world over the last 25 years. Let me reach out to that group before going to the expense of hiring a recruiting firm." It was a bold statement. Scott agreed, but now the burden reverted to me.

Task one for me at Fusion-io was to hire an extraordinary vice president of global sales. I needed a VP of sales who would reflect my personality to the sales force. We needed to work well as a team in tandem. People regarded me as an enthusiastic, action-oriented communicator. I was not, however, a technology visionary. I had an extraordinary one in David Flynn, founder of the company, so I did not need my VP of sales to be a deep technologist. Rather, I absolutely needed someone who understood our market, who knew how to build a sales team, and who knew how to knock down some doors.

We needed someone who knew how to sell to the Chief Information Officers at places like Goldman Sachs, Bloomberg, Facebook, Apple, and Credit-Suisse. We needed someone who had the credibility and the skills to tell the smartest guys on the planet that the way they had architected their data centers was upside down and should be rethought. And we needed someone with the guts to do it while representing a tiny, Utah-based company which, at the time, had a mere 60 employees.

So, I turned to LinkedIn and posted the following message: "Who is the best IT Sales VP on planet Earth?"

Scott McKinley saw my post. Scott and I had met in the late 90's when he was running a Utah-based venture capital fund. Scott was sharp. He had a world of experience working at investment banks. In particular, he had spent a substantial part of his career working in the Asia-Pacific region. When he saw my LinkedIn post, Scott emailed me directly at my Yahoo account. Now, I had not spoken to or seen Scott in approximately ten years. He had moved out of state and had started a university to train software programmers and technical people, called Neumont University.

Despite the separation and distance, I had remembered Scott as someone with great intelligence and connections.

Happily, Scott wrote to me and suggested I contact someone by the name of Jim Dawson. He said something to the effect that he ran sales for a data storage company called "Par 3, or something like that." I initially thought Jim must work for a golf company, but then I realized that Scott had been referring to 3Par, a data storage company based in the San Francisco Bay area. I was excited to connect with Jim, since 3Par was squarely in our marketplace.

I immediately dove into Google to learn more about Jim and his company. I learned that the company was based in Fremont, California. I guessed at Jim's email address and sent him a message.

February 2009

Jim - How are you doing? Scott McKinley recommended I contact you. I am the CEO of Fusion-io. Looks like you are running the sales organization at 3Par. Congrats on your successes there. We have some great things going on at Fusion-io, highlighted yesterday with the announced partnership with HP and a little earlier with Steve Wozniak, inventor of the Apple, joining us as our Chief Scientist. I happen to be in the Bay Area for 2 days if you would care to chat. I would enjoy visiting with you in person or by phone. My cell is 801-995-1348.

Warm Regards, David B

Note some of the techniques I used to get Jim to stand up and take action on an unsolicited email. This is what I mean about working smart. First, I used a mutual friend for the referral. I made sure that Jim knew the email was coming from a reasonably credible source (i.e., CEO of Fusion-io). It was important to me that I complimented him as having been the main man running sales at 3Par. The tone was friendly, not formal. I offered to meet him personally. This would make it convenient for him. Even though I had never met Jim, I gave him my personal cell number. I gave him reasons that Fusion-io was a happening place and included some press on an HP deal we had struck, as well as the reference to Steve Wozniak, our Chief Scientist.

As we look at this "Work Hard" principle, it is important to note that what I did here was not difficult. It was not heavy lifting, physically strenuous, or necessarily demanding of my time. However, this is where you must look at work differently and see networking in a new light. Networking well, by utilizing your connections and prioritizing your relationships, can yield great results. Implementing skills such as noticing others' accomplishments and figuring out ways to connect may offer valuable avenues to those who can come alongside you and up both of your games dramatically.

A few things that I learned about Jim Dawson during our initial meetings and phone calls:

1. He loves sports
2. He lives in the San Francisco Bay Area
3. He is a member of the LDS faith

Learning these three things about Jim immediately made me think of Steve Young. I don't know anyone with those three characteristics who does not idolize Steve—and he was on the Fusion-io advisory board. I was excited to make the connection for Jim. On my next trip to the Bay Area, I went to Dick's Sporting Goods and bought a special football—one with a specific place for an autograph. I then went right over to Steve's home and asked him to sign it and add a personalized note:

"To Jim Dawson and Family - Fusion-io - Go for it - Best Regards, Steve Young"

That was on a Friday. The very next day, I went to a FedEx office, boxed up the football, and express mailed it to Jim's home in Orinda, California, just outside San Francisco. As Jim would later tell me, his wife unwrapped the package while Jim was at his office at 3Par. She immediately called Jim, ecstatic about this personally autographed football. Then she asked, "Jim, what's Fusion-io?" Jim explained to her that he had been discussing a potential job offer with me. Her reply? "You gotta join that company!"

Jim did join our company, and Fusion-io became the beneficiary of his amazing sales skills and management talent. In fact, in the January-March quarter of 2010 (six months after Dawson arrived), the company's revenues were $12 million. A year later, for the same quarter, they exceeded $66 million. The impact that a great VP of Sales can have on an organization is inestimable.

Work with Your End in Mind

As Jim would later tell the story, he remembers the dogged persistence I had displayed in trying to hire him. He claims he told me, "Thanks, but I am not interested" at least three times.

Honestly, I don't remember ever hearing Jim tell me "No!" I guess that is my very point. Work with your end in mind, and don't settle for second best. Create your own self-fulfilling prophecy and then work hard to realize that goal.

After Jim Dawson joined Fusion-io, I went to Uinta Golf, a golf equipment store located in Salt Lake City, and bought Scott McKinley the best driver I could find in the shop. One thing I knew about Scott from our interactions years earlier was that Scott loved to play golf. Scott's connection and willingness to take the time to reach out and share that resource with me when I needed it literally changed the trajectory of Fusion-io. I wanted to show him how much I appreciated his lead that day.

Make the Law of Reciprocity Work for You

The lesson in all of this for me is simply this: You may not know the right people with the right answers right now. But you may know people who know them. They may put you in touch with one key individual who can change your business or personal life in one email. While it may seem simple, it is some of the best hard work you can do.

As I was able to get to know Jim better, I learned that he had grown up in Ogden, Utah, before relocating to the Bay Area. He loved to fish. On one of our very early encounters, Jim told me of a personal goal he had to buy a place on the Madison River in Montana, known as one of the great trout fishing streams in the world. I promised Jim, at that time, to do everything I could to try and help him achieve that goal. I am happy to report that just before Christmas 2010, Jim bought that place on the Madison. Fusion-io gave him plenty of opportunities to fulfill his dreams and use his skills. He blessed the lives of many at Fusion-io through his leadership, the great teams he has built, and the results he has achieved. This is the law of reciprocity in action.

Points to remember about working smart:

1. Use your LinkedIn connections to find new talent.
2. Show up. Be there in person whenever possible.
3. Get to know people personally. A signed football from Steve Young was important to Jim, while a golf club was the appropriate gift for Scott.
4. Stay in touch. Despite the fact that it had been over ten years since I had seen Scott McKinley, I had stayed in touch, which yielded incredible results.

Work Smart using Social Media

Every morning, I wake up and prioritize my day. Usually I have a list of the 20 or 30 things that I want to achieve that day. As I look over my list, I do a sanity check and ask myself, "Which of these is most important? What things must I accomplish today? Do I need to hire someone today? Is there a contract I must finalize? Is there a connection I need to make to establish a position on an advisory board? What takes precedence?" With so many things that I am responsible for, and people to whom I am responsible, I must determine which priorities come first.

The hardest work for any of us is the proper use of our personal capital. The decisions on how and where to allocate your time are an essential part of working smart. Personal capital also goes to your character. Where you spend your time is a reflection of what is driving you at your core. The more you display characteristics of integrity and purpose in allocating your daily activities, the greater your ability to succeed. I often say to myself, "Don't let the things that matter the least get in the way of things that matter the most."

You cannot afford to let the trivial get in the way of the real substance of things you need to accomplish.

Some might dismiss the use of social media as not substantive, but I contend it is essential to communicating and staying in touch in the twenty-first century. Are you working hard to incorporate social media platforms as part of your daily habit? In my view, there is real substance in the smart use of social media.

Plan effectively, delegate strategically, and prioritize your relationships with networking at the forefront. As you plan your day, plan as well for building upon and deepening your relationships. It is through your relationships that many of your goals can be achieved.

The power of networking enables you to have much greater efficiency in the way you conduct and drive your business and personal objectives. Let me share with you my list from a typical day in late 2012:

- Get stats on State of Utah
- Review list of To Do's from meeting with IGC
- Review Linda's Executive Summary for her Virtual Immersive Educational World
- Figure board possibilities
- Call Robin Ferracone
- Check on travel plans with the kids
- Give Linda Times and Seasons artwork
- Wash dishes and make dinner
- Respond to LinkedIn and Facebook friends' requests
- Send Patcee photos of mission call
- Call Greg Butterfield
- Email Matt Christensen, re: meeting up week after next
- Email Lowell Anderson
- Post notice on LinkedIn looking for Sales Reps
- Read article on Reed Hoffman in Forbes and send him a note
- Write up "Leaving a Legacy" and the story of Captain Elwin Pulsipher
- Read FAQ's on OpenVue. Let's be crisper moving forward and get all constituencies involved.
- Call Shawn Lindquist
- Email V-3 folks a thank-you note for the meeting
- Send feedback on our HireVue process to the team
- Read scriptures
- Quote for the day for Facebook: "A sale is not something you pursue. It is something that happens while you are immersed in serving the customer." Tweet, as well.
- Read documents relative to Series C including Schedule of Exceptions

- Follow up on Donny Osmond note
- Talk to Phil, re: term sheet and the board moving forward

Some of the items on my "To-Do" list are gathering details or completing specific tasks. However, if you look closely at the list, many of the items are rooted in a relationship—either initiating a relationship or maintaining it. Even washing the dishes is a relationship piece, because it will strengthen the relationship with my wife, who asked me to help. Ultimately, to be effective and satisfied in your life, your top priority must be nurturing the relationships around you and connecting with a team of individuals that synergistically impact mutual goals.

Refer to your own "To-Do" list. Are you prioritizing your relationships? Are you making time for the phone calls and in-person visits that will build your network and ultimately your life? Are you scheduling time for the growth you wish to see in your business connections and associations? Add time to your networking luncheons to arrive early and stay later. Set aside time each week to send personalized notes to those who deserve praise. Thank the people who serve you and serve with you. Notice the special events that are going on in the lives of those with whom you associate, and find ways to congratulate them sincerely and genuinely. In addition, make time for the relationships that come before business, such as family and spirituality. These relationships are the petri dish for real personal growth.

Give It All You've Got

As you look around for possible team members, look for those who display passion and determination. These qualities will be essential as you grow a company, an alliance, or a brand. Look at candidates' skill sets. What do they offer? How do they engage with others? How do they go after their own goals and purposes? Observe how possible team members exert themselves in other areas of their lives and how these same skills can benefit your objectives. Surround yourself with people who give it all they've got and put their heart and soul in the game.

In 1992, Linda and I moved into a new area of Provo, Utah. We had built a lovely home on the Provo River in a neighborhood called "The Woods at Riverside." Ours was the third home in this new development. Shortly after our house was built, the Weekes family began to build a very impressive home nearby. As we attended the same church congregation, we became close friends with Brad and Stephanie Weekes, as well as their parents, Mel and Bonnie Hammond, and Stephanie's sister, Natalie. As time passed, we were introduced to Natalie's soon-to-be husband, Shawn Lindquist.

As the years passed, we often crossed paths with Natalie and Shawn. In fact, on several occasions, I made it a point to be there for the births of several of their children. (I showed up.) Shawn played NCAA basketball for the BYU Cougars, and I was mesmerized by his skill. I had played basketball many years earlier in Red Lodge, Montana, and I was an avid fan of BYU Basketball. At 6'5" Shawn was one of the most tenacious defenders I had ever seen on the basketball court. He was the guy that no one wanted to play against because of his willingness to do the hard work on the basketball court that nobody else was willing to do.

Shawn carried this skill with him as he progressed in life. As the years passed, I continued to see his tenacity play out in his personal life and accomplishments at work. In 2010, Shawn joined Fusion-io as my senior vice president and chief legal counsel. At his arrival in 2010, critical litigation was ongoing, as previous employees saw Fusion's success and wanted a piece of it. The claims involved complicated intellectual property issues, company stock options, and arguments about employee performance. People on both sides were convinced of the correctness of their position. To say the litigation was "heated" would be an understatement. I knew that if Fusion-io were to ever become the success we were hoping for, we needed to put this mess behind us. It would require someone of sterling character, unmatched work ethic, a stellar reputation in the legal community, and a dynamic personality to make it happen. That was a pretty accurate description of Shawn Lindquist.

Shawn Lindquist's amazing capacity for work set him apart. He has blessed the lives of many through the lessons of hard work he learned early in his life that stay with him to this day. He grew up in a family with almost nothing. He was the son of a single mother at the bottom of the food chain economically. He had it tough growing up, and the likelihood of his success was doubtful. Nevertheless, Shawn overcame a thousand obstacles that could have held him back. He took the tough path after his successful collegiate basketball career and persevered through law school. I hired him as an intern to work in our legal department at Novell. He performed amazingly well. But Shawn wanted more. He asked me for an introduction to one of the most prestigious law firms on the planet: Wilson, Sonsini, Goodrich, and Rosati. I knew that they typically only hired graduates from Cal, Stanford, or Harvard (he had attended Brigham Young University), but Shawn was determined to "get in there." I knew it would be useless to discourage Shawn from trying to go with this big-time law firm.

Despite my misgivings, I introduced him to the managing partner, Larry Sonsini. Shawn's tenacity and skill showed up admirably there, and he was given a job as a young associate in the firm. He went on to make partner. Among other things, he helped write the book on taking companies public. Some years later, he returned to Utah, became general counsel for Omniture, and helped to take them public. We were then extremely fortunate at Fusion-io to become the beneficiary of Shawn's work ethic and commitment. In June of 2011, Fusion-io achieved its

Initial Public Offering on the New York Stock Exchange, due in no small part to Mr. Lindquist.

Because of his 20 years of dedication to the law craft prior to joining Fusion-io, and his work in developing a specific expertise in taking companies public (after all, he wrote a book on that very subject), Shawn Lindquist became a real difference maker. By sheer hard work and persistence, Shawn not only upped his own game, but also brought a number of people along for the ride.

Shawn Lindquist is a great example of what Vinod Khosla once said, "It is not the *what*, but the *who*." People are the difference-makers. Shawn is a difference maker. While technology is important, people supply the energy, dynamics, and intelligence to drive superior results. It is like the computer itself. You can pack a computer full of RAM, SSD's, and software—but unless there are some very smart humans operating that computer, you will not generate the results you hope for.

Look for talent. Look for tenacity. Look for those who by their very nature give it all they've got.

Build a Killer Team

Every CEO has his or her strengths. Some are brilliant with technology; others are great at execution; still others have the gift of vision. But they all know one thing: the key to working smart is to build an amazing team. As Gary Halbert stated, "Most people spend 90 percent of their time on what they're not best at [and] only 10 percent of their time on their best ability. Successful people delegate that 90 percent [and] are thus able to spend all their time on their 'unique' ability." One of my core strengths just happens to be connecting people. I have capitalized on that strength in my CEO roles because it was the thing I had a passion for and was best at. Again, it is not the *what* but the *who*. You can have an "A" product, but if it is surrounded by only a "C" management team, then the enterprise is doomed to failure. On the other hand, give a "C" product to an "A" management team, and even the least interesting products have a chance. Build a killer team, and you will see unprecedented results. In essence, I believe a key role for any CEO is to be his company's Chief Talent Officer.

With the addition of Jim Dawson, Shawn Lindquist, and Steve Wozniak, along with additional salespeople, Fusion-io was beginning to hum. It was an exciting time. The exponential growth we were all hoping for was happening. This created a new need. We needed a Chief Financial Officer (CFO) who could not only account for the money flows, but also one who had a broad vision and a strategic mindset. I realized that Fusion-io actually had what it took to do an Initial Public Offering. But that would require someone with more than just a run-of-the-mill CFO background. We needed someone who had talked to the Wall Street types before. We also needed an individual who knew what it was like to do a "bake-off" with investment bankers. A "bake-off" is simply a series of meetings with a variety of investment banks to determine which of them will lead your public offering. So, of course, I turned to social media.

One morning, in my Facebook update box, I posted the following question: "Who is the best public company CFO you know?"

After a couple of days, George Boutros posted a comment on my wall that read: "Do you know Dennis Wolf, former CFO of MySQL? He sold his last company to Sun Microsystems for a billion dollars."

George and I had interacted in the late 80's and early 90's when Novell was doing a series of public offerings. At the time, George was working at Morgan Stanley. He worked closely with Frank Quattrone, and together they had a string of similar successes at Deutsch Bank and Credit Suisse. I had always liked George as an investment banker. He was sharp, honest, and responsive. He was also a connection of mine on LinkedIn and Facebook. When George recommended Dennis, I was immediately interested.

Plus, it was clear that Dennis had experience in high tech on the financial side. This was not an easy blend to find.

I didn't have a current email address, so I sent George a message using Facebook, and we began an illuminating exchange. George expressed his excitement over the things that he had heard about Fusion-io from one Hylton Van Zyl at Credit Suisse. (See chapter one for more on Hylton.) He added: "It sounds like you have a tiger by the tail. I hope we can connect in person soon."

I proceeded to ask more about Dennis Wolf. I learned that not only had Dennis Wolf worked at MySQL, but also at Apple Computer. What put me over the top in terms of my interest level was that Dennis was on the board of directors of Quantum, one of the world's largest data storage companies. He was an awesome fit for our growing data storage company.

After reading Dennis's bio, I was determined to meet this man in person. Several weeks later, I went over to Silicon Valley and brought Dennis into our Fusion offices there. We hit it off immediately. I could tell this was a man of integrity. Before hiring Dennis, I called his former boss, the man who had been the CEO of MySQL, Marten Mickos. Marten spent substantial time singing his praises.

We hired Dennis, and he became another key component of the Fusion-io success story. It would not have happened but for the hard work I had done over the years nurturing a large personal network and through the smart use of social media. Without a key Facebook post and "staying in touch" over time with George, this critical hire for Fusion-io would never have happened. Build your social network well and with credibility, and you will have access to the resources for team building at the moment you have a need.

By the way, I think it is important to note that building relationships is about constantly being kind, giving, and nurturing to people who are contributing to your success. Dennis

Wolf performed magnificently for Fusion, so I did my best to reciprocate. When Dennis asked me if I could help his daughters find jobs, I immediately opened up my network to him and was able to line up job discussions for his daughters in places like Symantec, Cisco, and SuperMicro. In my mind, it is all about relationship nurturing through mutual support.

Building a killer team is not only important on the management level, but it also applies to building strong advisory boards. Advisory boards can play a big role in bringing talent to the table. That talent leverages the leadership in proportion to the desired growth and multiplies the results a hundredfold. Bringing individuals to the table with diversified skill sets and their own networks and connections multiplies your reach and your possibilities. This applies not just to companies but also to individuals. As you read through my advice on building a company advisory board, think too about the way this can help you build your personal board of advisors.

As you look at someone to be on your advisory board, realize that you are providing them with some real benefits. For example, they will be interacting with other people who have been very successful in their careers. It will be another networking opportunity for them. The people that served on the advisory board at Fusion-io were automatically connected to Steve Wozniak and Steve Young: two important connections. You will also want to give them stock in the company to ensure their ongoing interest in its growth. Many advisory board members I have worked with also get excited about the technology or innovations and want to be onboard to see those innovations move forward.

My current position is the Executive Chairman of HireVue, a digital interviewing platform that expedites the hiring process through the use of online interviewing programs. One of our advisory board members is Larry King. This was a natural fit, as Larry King is known as the greatest interviewer of all time.

Larry and his wife, Shawn, had asked me to review some of their prospective business engagements. I was happy to do it without a thought of remuneration. They graciously offered to reciprocate with anything I needed, as well. A couple of months later, I asked Larry to join a strategic advisory board at HireVue. We were thrilled to have him. This led to Shawn and her brother Paul asking me to assist them with another potentially game-changing company called "The Business Campus." Connections lead to more connections, and building an awesome advisory board allows you to grow your greatest resource pool.

As you build your synergistic teams, here are ten ways an advisory board can help you.

1. **Leads you to future potential permanent board members:** You can see early on who has passion for the business and who will help you carry the load.

2. **Offers key account introductions:** Referrals here may come from active advisory board members through association.

3. **Offers funding recommendations:** Most of your advisors have been through this drill many times and will have thoughts on the timing of funding and connections to funding sources.

4. **Lends credibility to your company:** "Surround yourself with greatness," as Chad Lewis writes in his book of the same title.

5. **Fills gaps in your management team:** If you lack technical expertise in an area, bring in an advisor who has knowledge in your weaker areas. Advisory board members can act as highly paid talent in exchange for some stock options. Imagine what it would cost to hire the skill and experience of those on the Fusion-io advisory board.

6. **Limits legal exposure for advisors:** Many former executives prefer being members of an advisory board, as it does not impose the level of legal obligations that are associated with being a member of the company's formal board of directors.

7. **Helps in recruiting top talent to the company**: By using the Rolodexes of senior operating professionals in the industry, your company will gain access to key potential employees.

8. **Offers competitive intelligence:** Proper advisory board members will have widespread insight into what is going on in the industry and what the competitors are up to. They can also act as a sounding board to determine how a particular company initiative might resonate in the marketplace before you go through the time and expense of implementation.

9. **Limits cost and expense:** The fees and stock options associated with advisory boards are generally small relative to your ROI (return on investment) and are clearly lower than such fees or options you would pay to formal board members who have fiduciary obligations to the company. Typically, informal meetings are held once or twice a year, and yet you have access year-round to the expertise of the advisors by virtue of a single phone call.

10. **Creates mentoring:** It is a great thing to have willing and informed advisors. In many instances, your advisors will have previously dealt with some of the more dicey situations you may encounter as a leader. Smart advisory board members can act as a personal sounding board to guide you on which ideas to pursue and how to spend your capital.

Your goal in building your advisory board should be to create an interactive group of highly talented professionals that can support you as your career moves ahead. It is essential in building your connections to find those people who have talents and resources that will add credibility to your cause and maturity to your pool of thought. Attract an anchor, mentor, or advisor like a Steve Wozniak, a Steve Young, or a Larry King, and you will find your level of value in the marketplace will increase exponentially. Find those within your industry who can open more doors, nurture more relationships, and grow more depth in the networks you are building. But make no mistake, it takes someone who is working hard and working smart to build out a world-class group of advisors.

So I will ask . . . Are you working hard, working smart, and utilizing social media to Up Your Game?

CHAPTER 8 GAME PLAN

1. Remember that creating and nurturing a world-class network takes hard work. Do not shy away from it. Do something every day to expand and organize your network. But make no mistake, the word "work" is in "network" for a reason. It takes commitment and real effort.

2. Remember that networking is like preparing for any athletic contest. It requires consistent and daily work on the effort.

3. Work smart by using the power of crowdsourcing on Twitter, Facebook, LinkedIn, and other platforms to attract talent to your company with simple postings.

4. Build a killer advisory board team. Members of that team will have previously dealt with the dicey situations in the workplace. Look to them as a personal sounding board.

5. Provide leads to your own network of people. When you hear of board positions, projects, groups, or business leads, take the time to tell others about them. Most people don't.

6. Working smart includes the broad crowdsourcing of information to solve today's problems in business. The broader and deeper your network, the more quickly and efficiently you can overcome obstacles in your business.

SIX TIMELESS PRINCIPLES THAT CAN DEFINITIVELY UP YOUR GAME

As more and more noise enters the media and technology space, the greatest challenge will be to find genuine, sincere connections. With the barrage of social media platforms out there, people must daily, even hourly, filter through the clutter of nonessential spam in all its forms and choose the forums and messages that mean the most to them personally. *The single best way to get someone's attention is to develop a sincere, one-on-one relationship.* The best way to drive to the top of any organization is to build relationships of trust with real people. At the end of the day, it is our relationships that impact us most in life. *Our relationships create the legacy we leave.*

It is the personal nature of relationships that differentiates the noise from the meaningful. One day, while sitting at my office at HireVue, I heard a spontaneous eruption of cheering and applause. Staff rallied around and whooped and hollered.

Dan, a new employee just two weeks on the job, had made his first sale. Now, the sale itself with regard to dollar value was not significant. However, the personal victory *was*. A blast email was sent company-wide. Dan was overwhelmingly recognized for his first close, with over a third of the company sending personal emails of congratulations. Even in a group dynamic, such as the corporate culture at HireVue, it is still the power of individual connection that makes our lives memorable. It is also those personal connections that can ensure our success in our personal and professional lives.

Let me restate as I've done throughout this book: The key to upping your game is to build genuine relationships with the smart use of technology. And let me just add a word or two about the word "networking." It is time this word stopped getting a bad rap. Networking, simply stated, is doing everything you can on a regular basis to secure and expand your personal relationships in order to increase the likelihood for success—your own success and the success of others. Through the benefits of technology, your networking reach can be wider and deeper than ever before. Your goal in networking should never be about growing the *numbers* of people to whom you are connected but rather the depth of those connections.

In my mind, networking is simply the need we all have to support one another. I often think of the story of the California Redwood trees. They are the oldest living things on planet Earth, reaching heights of greater than an entire football field. They are subjected to some of the most difficult weather on Earth. One of their most fascinating characteristics is that their root systems only go down *six inches* into the ground. How in the world do these immense giants stand for thousands of years despite wind, ice, and snow with roots that are merely half a foot underground? What possibly holds them up? The answer is simply this: Their root systems, while incredibly shallow, expand outward for hundreds of yards and intertwine with one another. In other words, a giant forest of redwood trees remains standing because the trees are linked, or networked, together.

One of my personal heroes is John Wooden, the legendary UCLA basketball coach. I was a basketball fanatic in the 1960's and was a three-year starter on my high school varsity team. I observed and watched UCLA closely for all of the years Wooden coached the Bruins. His record of winning the NCAA Championships 10 times with UCLA is unprecedented. But in his life, Wooden always emphasized the nature of connecting with people around you to form a great team. He knew the importance of building and maintaining trusting relationships not just with his players, but also with his coaching peers. He would tell others that "friendship is a fine art" and that "friends are essential in your journey to success and significance."

If you are willing to take the time to utilize today's online social mediums while, even more importantly, taking a genuine interest in other people's lives and careers, your own personal roots will expand outward and become intertwined with hundreds if not thousands of others. The value of your network will grow exponentially.

I have observed that people who rise to the top of their professions are motivated by the desire to help other people. My old boss at Novell, the great Ray Noorda, remarked many times that his greatest joy in life was providing jobs and meaningful work for those around him.

Indeed, the greatest leaders, in the long run, are those individuals who care first about others. They lead with a higher purpose.

The great leader Andrew Carnegie once said: "No man will make a great leader who wants to do it all himself, or to get all the credit for doing it."

By following the six principles I have outlined in this book, you will be able to differentiate yourself from the noise, nurture real relationships, and truly Up Your Game. Implementing even one of the principles here has the ability to radically change the outcomes of your connections. Implementing all six can forever change the results you are having professionally and relationally. The six Up Principles have made me a better father, a better leader, a better connector, a better business partner, and a better man. As I reflect on each of the six principles, I am struck by the impact others have had on my life as they have demonstrated each of these timeless characteristics.

Start Up Your Game by Giving

One of the greatest examples of personal impact comes from a man who was known by only a few. When I met him, Captain Elwin Pulsipher, a former war hero and military leader in Vietnam, was in the later stages of ALS, or Lou Gehrig's disease. He was confined to a bed and barely had the use of his fingers. Almost completely paralyzed, the only parts of his body that he could move regularly were his eyelids. Nonetheless, his mind was still sharp, and he was still imbued with a deep desire to serve others. By contrast, at this time in my life, I was pretty focused on myself. My father had just passed away, we had moved our young family from Southern California to Utah, and I had just transitioned to a new job. But when I met Elwin, he helped change my thinking from inward to outward. This great man and former leader was all about giving with no thought of getting.

On a weekly basis, despite overwhelming odds against it, Elwin sent personal letters to ten missionaries from our church congregation who were serving around the globe. The process was difficult and painful. *It took hours for him to write just one.* His family connected electrodes to his eyelids and, as he would blink, a cursor on his computer would move to each letter in the alphabet. Blink by blink, he would create a letter, then a word, and then a paragraph. I visited him monthly and interacted with him as best I could as he shared his efforts to support the missionaries. He sacrificed greatly to encourage and share his faith, and the missionaries—and I—were profoundly impacted by his service. In my mind, the most successful networks are those that are established by giving people like Captain Pulsipher. So when you start up your network, start with an attitude of giving first.

People *think* about connecting. They *think* to contact a friend about the loss of his job *or think* to congratulate another buddy on his latest adventure or a sister on a move or a friend on a graduation. They think of giving of their time and materials to others. These thoughts are often fleeting, and the opportunity to connect is often missed. But *the people who make a difference in the world are those people who act on those fleeting thoughts and carry a positive message into the world.*

Show Up and Up Your Game

As a teenager, my thinking was profoundly influenced by my best friend in high school, Jim Patenaude. He and I loved sports and played on our city and high school teams together. At the beginning of my senior year of high school in Montana, my father became ill, and it was necessary for my parents to move away from our home in Red Lodge. But I wanted to finish my senior year there. It was at that critical juncture in my life that Jim Patenaude showed up for me. He was the first to reach out a hand and offer sympathy for our family's misfortune. He went so far as to invite me to live in his home for the entire 1969 class year. He showed up for me emotionally as well as in person. Jim was my biggest cheerleader on the basketball court.

I moved in with Jim for that last year. I observed how Jim chose to live differently than the "cool crowd." He was a stand-up guy in every way. My father and some of my siblings had gone down a path that was riddled with challenges. I remember the pain it gave my mother, and I didn't want to bring her any more pain. I also knew that in order to be successful in life, I would need to avoid those behaviors or they could destroy my life. My best friend, Jim, and my mother helped me navigate those difficult teenage years. Their impact upon me was profound and set the course for the rest of my life. They showed up for me when I needed it most.

Follow Up and Up Your Game

One of the best examples of someone that follows up is Scott Cutler, executive vice president of the New York Stock Exchange. I met Scott when he was a young investment banker back in the early 2000's. Since then, I have watched his career blossom in magnificent ways. One of the reasons for Scott's success is his ability to follow up with immediacy. I cannot think of a time over the years of our interactions when it took more than a day to hear back from Scott on any issue. This is true despite the fact that Scott has a large family, is an active member of the Young Presidents' Organization, is Vice Chairman of the Board of the NYC Mental Health Association, is a board member of the Council of the Americas and the British American Business Council, and holds important roles in his church.

Scott is a great example of the adage: "When you want something done, ask a busy person." From golf outings to political fundraisers to events on the floor of the New York Stock Exchange, Scott is always there and always following up. So when Fusion-io was thinking about going public, we thought of Scott and could not envision going with any of the other exchanges. Scott made our experience of going public truly one of the most memorable days of my life by ensuring that all details were attended to. He also is careful to remember folks. In the summer of 2013, he invited me to a golf outing with Steve Stricker the day after the

PGA Golf championship. It was a great day . . . but then Scott went the extra mile. Within several weeks of the event held at Whistling Straits in Wisconsin, I received an absolutely gorgeous photobook from Scott containing dozens of photos of the day.

Today, I am involved with another company that has an IPO as a possible dream—HireVue. Do you think I would recommend going with anyone but the NYSE in connection with that IPO so long as Mr. Scott Cutler is there? No. Scott is part of that unique subset of businesspeople in the world that follow up on everything in a terrific way.

Link Up and Up Your Game

In the late 1990's, my boss at Novell was our then CEO Eric Schmidt. I served as Eric's Chief Legal Counsel at Novell for four years. We both left the company within roughly six months of each other in late 2000 and early 2001. It was a great run together. Eric Schmidt went on to become CEO of Google. While Eric did an excellent job at Novell, I always knew there was further greatness awaiting him. Eric was an outstanding example of someone who knew how to link up with others on more than just a surface level. I came to know early on that friends were very important to Eric. Once he knew you and trusted you, you became one of Eric's friends. Now, I look back on the last almost 20 years of knowing Eric, and I have appreciated how much it has meant to me, personally, to be a friend of Eric's. He taught me a lot about creating personal relationships and not just business ones. He also understood the concept that making connections needs to start long before you ever need anything.

One day, in 1997, I was sitting in my office. Eric swung by and got right down to business. "David," he said, "I want to host a dinner for Senator Orrin Hatch at my home in Silicon Valley." Now, knowing that Eric is a deeply committed Democrat, and knowing that Senator Hatch is an equally devout Republican, I thought, for an initial second, that he was kidding. I started to get a smile on my face but Eric quickly added, "I am quite serious. Do you think this is something you would like to do? Can you help me pull it together?" Of course, I replied with a big "yes." A couple of months later, there we were at Eric's home in the heart of the Silicon Valley with our Democrat CEO thanking Republican Senator Hatch profusely for all that he had done to support the technology industries over the years (which, by the way, was very well deserved).

I could tell from the interchange of those two giants that night that they had become fast friends. As a direct result of Eric's foresight and intuition, an important relationship was secured and a mutual admiration society began. Some ten years later, I was asked to emcee a night with Eric hosted by the Utah Technology Council at the Grand America Hotel in Salt Lake City. It was Senator Hatch who asked Eric to revisit our fair state that night. It was a rousing success.

What is significant about Eric's relationship building is that it begins years, perhaps decades, before he needs it. In fact, Senator Hatch may have never reciprocated, and that would have been OK with Eric. But my guess is that Eric and Orrin's relationship has benefited each of them brilliantly over the years.

Contrary to the idea that "it's not personal, it's just business," Eric Schmidt understood the value of a deep and trusting personal relationship, and it has manifested itself in Eric's brilliant work in the business world.

Stand Up and Up Your Game

In 1972, as I returned to college from an LDS mission in France, I read Stephen R. Covey's book entitled *Spiritual Roots of Human Relations*. I was moved by the basic concept of the book that all of our relationships (the stuff that we have discussed in this book) are spiritual in nature. It addresses the roots of relationship problems and suggests spiritual solutions, such as vision, commitment, understanding, example, communication, and self-discipline. Covey also underscored the importance of integrity, as illustrated by the life of Sir Thomas More.

Thomas More was a brilliant jurist in Renaissance England who served in parliament and on diplomatic missions. Unlike most royal servants in that day, he had unimpeachable integrity. He could not be bribed. He believed, above all else, in the fairness and supremacy of the rule of law. As a member of parliament and later as Chancellor of England, he worked industriously to promote justice and faith in the courts. However, he resigned in 1532 when King Henry VIII was determined to annul his marriage to Catherine of Aragon. The king also wanted to disassociate himself from the Catholic Church and start the Church of England. Eventually, More was given the option to either compromise his integrity and support the king—or die. He chose the latter. In other words, he was a stand-up person.

Though we will not all be faced with life-and-death decisions such as this, when our decisions in life are taken in total, they do determine the sum of our life's accomplishments and how we will be memorialized in death. Successful leaders and those who win in the game of life learn early on the importance of standing up for what is right. In other words, integrity means everything.

Scale Up and Up Your Game

Scaling up your world-class network takes time, hard work, and commitment. I set aside time every day to get better connected with people via social media as well as in physical venues from work to speaking engagements to the golf course. But make no mistake . . it takes conscientious thought, persistence, and organization to get it done.

Until I was ten, I attended Central Elementary School in Burbank, California. I still have fond memories of those childhood years. My best friend back then was Paul Phinney. Our family moved from Burbank, California, to Montana during my fourth grade year, and my hope of ever connecting with Paul Phinney was small. However, as a result of working to build my network through LinkedIn, I was recently able to reconnect with this now older gentleman with whom I had not spoken in over 50 years. As it turns out, my good buddy Paul Phinney became a medical doctor of some distinction. He recently served as the President of the California Medical Association. What a thrill it was to reconnect after all of those years.

Interestingly, Central Elementary School was later renamed Walt Disney Elementary because of the great career of Mr. Disney and the fact that much of the Disney corporation flourished right there in Burbank. However, most people don't know that this great business leader suffered numerous setbacks in his career. The truth is that it took him ten years after establishing his company before his first success, Mickey Mouse, took off. Walt once said: "All the adversity I have had in my life . . . has strengthened me. You may not realize it when it appears, but a kick in the teeth may be the best thing in the world for you."

Stated another way, every person goes through tough times, especially when they are chasing a big dream. But the ones who eventually win have the tenacity to keep going.

When I think of hard work and commitment, I know of no better example than my companion of 40 years, Dr. Linda Marie Bradford. Neither one of us grew up with much of anything. But Linda, through sheer hard work and determination, is a Ph.D. in Instructional Technology and Psychology and also holds a master's degree in Art Education. This she achieved while fighting an illness that has plagued her for over 30 years—Fibromyalgia. Linda is a magnificent example of the statement made many years ago by C.S. Lewis, who said: "You are never too old to set another goal or to dream a new dream."

In 1981, Linda was hit with a virus that was completely debilitating—something called Cytomegalovirus. She was pregnant with our fourth child, and she essentially could not move out of her bed for six months. The virus was one that could also damage the fetus of our little baby, and it was a very scary time for both of us. Through much prayer, our little baby, Angela, not only survived but thrived. Linda, despite her inability to move out of her sick bed for more than an hour or two a day, actually began to perfect the art of calligraphy. Calligraphy is the art of beautiful handwriting and involves a number of different styles and intricacies. Stated another way, it ain't easy. Linda had learned some basic skills a few years earlier from her church friend, Kathy. But now, faced with months of complete bed rest, instead of feeling sorry for herself, she worked on her calligraphy and became a world-class expert in this art form.

The artwork she has created over the decades and the gifts she has given to many are treasures in our home and in the homes of dozens. Further, in 1984, Linda was selected to be one of the elite calligraphers for the Olympic Games based in Los Angeles, California. In that role, she penned elegant and timeless personalized invitations to attend the games to dignitaries around the globe.

So when I think of feeling defeated or not being able to follow through on something, I think of my awesome bride and what she has overcome to become a world-class calligrapher. Further, using her Ph.D. studies, she formed her own company—the V.I.E.W.—Virtual Immersive Educational World. With her passion for education, she is driving a revolution in online education. The VIEW is a cloud-based 3D educational learning environment that allows any educational institution to expand their influence digitally instead of physically. She and her team of developers have created dozens of 3D learning platforms.

All of this from a young lady that has struggled with health issues for more than three-fourths of our married life. Yes . . . when I think of scaling up to Up Your Game through hard work and persistence, Linda is a preeminent example.

Measure Your Potential Impact on Others

Nothing will define you more than the people who impact your life at pivotal junctures. It is also true that your impact on others in their pivotal moments can never be underestimated. You may never realize how your words have encouraged growth, how your resources have lifted another's burdens, or what your actions have put into motion. As you work side by side with people, you too will develop deep, supportive, long-term friendships. Every principle we have discussed in this book is ultimately meant to draw you closer into supportive relationships with others. Strong relationships are the reason for all of the work, the organizing, the social media, and the networking. Ultimately, it is through relationships that you impact others. People will always remember how you made them feel.

In today's high-tech world, what you experience with others may take place on many platforms. In big and small ways you are impacting others. Every phone call, text, email, and tweet affects someone—and may affect the masses.

Throughout this book, I have emphasized the profound impact we can have when we couple technology with the skills of personal connection. At the end of the day, it is all about relationships. While I have given you the blueprint to developing a life-changing network, make sure to measure your success not by money but by the impact you have on others and the degree to which you become a positive influencer.

Growing a billion-dollar network is done step by step, personal connection by personal connection. It requires starting up, showing up, following up, linking up, standing up, and scaling up in order to make an impact and be a positive influence on others. Do this, and you will have Upped Your Game in a big way. Do this, and you can literally change the world.

CHAPTER 9 GAME PLAN

1. "If you ask for money, you will get advice; if you ask for advice, you will get money." Therefore, ask for advice from everyone. It won't always come back in the form of money, but people will appreciate the fact that you value their opinion.

2. Broaden your scope to connect with people internationally; there will be another 1.2 billion people on the planet by 2025, but only 3 percent of that global growth will come from the United States and Europe.

3. Sit in the front row at an event. I sat in the front row of a speech given by Steve Wozniak, inventor of the Apple computer, some years ago. It led to my meeting his executive assistant, which led to a meeting with Steve, which led to his working for me.

4. Today's online access to people's professional backgrounds through Google searches, Facebook, and LinkedIn brings new transparency. Build your online persona in a way that demonstrates that you are a stand-up person with a positive outlook on life and one who is committed to helping others.

5. Make yourself available to others. Tell your friends, managers, and colleagues that you are interested in participating the next time a project comes up.

6. There is a revolutionary way of getting things done and finding solutions—brought to us courtesy of social media and commerce that has swept the digital world. Use it!

INDEX

D

David Checketts 53, 54, 94, 95, 96, 97
David Eric Bradford 77
David Fretz 61, 62
Deborah Day 80
Deepak Chopra 45
Dennis Wolf 162, 163
Dunbar's number 8

E

Eloqua 104, 116
Elwin Pulsipher 157, 172
emotional DNA 92
Eric Schmidt 1, 4, 84, 85, 97, 134, 135, 175, 176
Erin Schurtz 111
Everyone Social 104

F

Facebook 16, 17, 19, 20, 22, 23, 24, 26, 29, 32, 36, 37, 38, 40, 43, 44, 45, 48, 50, 62, 75, 76,
    77, 86, 87, 88, 89, 91, 92, 96, 99, 101, 102, 103, 104, 108, 111, 112, 115, 116, 117,
    118, 119, 120, 122, 123, 128, 131, 133, 137, 138, 139, 140, 141, 142, 143, 145, 151,
    157, 162, 163
Follow Up v, 5, 7, 22, 48, 83, 86, 149, 174
Forbes 4, 107, 132, 157
Forest Gump 79
FourSquare 26
Frank Quattrone 96, 97, 162
Fusion-io 1, 5, 13, 15, 33, 34, 35, 45, 58, 68, 71, 72, 73, 74, 85, 99, 102, 110, 120, 136, 137,
    150, 152, 153, 154, 155, 159, 160, 162, 163, 164, 165, 174

G

Gary Halbert 161
Gary Kildall 76, 123, 124, 125, 126
George Boutros 162
George Carlin 40
giving 4, 7, 8, 14, 22, 23, 43, 51, 52, 53, 57, 58, 60, 62, 63, 65, 69, 118, 122, 133, 142, 148,
    163, 172, 173
giving with no thought of getting 7, 23, 51, 52, 58, 172
Graham Doxey 45

H

I

J

K

L

M

W

Wall Street Journal 4, 113
win-win relationships 8, 106, 109, 127
working hard 8, 133, 156, 167
working smart 8, 148, 155, 156, 161, 167

Y

YouTube 41, 111, 142

ACKNOWLEDGMENTS

To my consultants and advisors: I once read that "relationships run the world." They are also largely responsible for the creation of this book. I spent a lot of time and effort talking to hundreds about writing books and trying to identify the most talented individuals available to help make it happen. I am deeply grateful to each of you. In the end, you have become more to me than just professional consultants and advisors. You have become friends and a blessing in my life.

Amy Osmond Cook. She is a fantastic editor, a doctor of literature, one of my terrific book publishers, someone who will go out of her way to help others, a great mother, and a true difference maker.

Jayme Johnson and the Worthy Marketing Group. Jayme is a brilliant marketer and has put organization around my life. Many thanks to her for driving this forward and herding ants. She is kind, thoughtful, and the consummate professional.

Cheryl Conner. Cheryl has been a friend through thick and thin for over 25 years. I have known, admired, and worked with her from our earliest days together at Novell. She has become the definitive guru in the State of Utah for all things related to Tech and PR.

Troie Battles. She is a wonderful book publisher, business colleague, friend, and advisor.

Krystyl Baldwin. A true social media guru. Thanks to Agent K for making great connections for me and helping to organize my life during a critical period.

Diane Christensen LeFrandt and Debra Lund. They helped me understand the importance of building a platform.

Tiffany Berg. She helped me early on to organize my approach to the book and assisted with the initial text. She is an inspirational leader and book author herself.

To my children: God bless you for being my friends and great examples to me. Remember that children are the living messages we send to a time we will not see. May you all love one another and make those future times and your relationships with each other ones Linda and I would be proud of. Thank you to Angela, who always Starts Up by giving without a thought of getting; Trevor, who always Follows Up; David Eric, for being a Stand Up person in all times and all places; and Aimee, who knows how to Link Up with people in a personal way and always make them feel special. Thanks as well to each of their spouses: Mindee, Amy, and Chris.

To my 16 exceptional grandchildren: I once read that "the soul is healed by being with children." Whenever I am around you precious little ones, my soul is filled with joy. Thanks to Daniel, Malia, McKay, Joshua, Abby, Adam, Ashlynn, Nia, Kate, Sunny, Lucy, Ella, Moti, Mollee, and Maxwell.

To my family members: Thank you for being there for me since the beginning. I love you.

My mother, Kay Bradford. She is our family matriarch who, at the age of 90, continues to inspire thousands with her positive outlook on life. Because of my mother, I learned, "It's not what you know. It's who you know." She taught me that through putting out a positive aura, one can connect with just about anyone on the planet in a meaningful way.

My father, Sylvester Duncan Bradford. Although he died in 1985, his death brought me to Novell, which became a shining gem in my work experience. I still believe it must have been him who whispered in my ear as my guardian angel and told me to get off I-15 that day and just "show up" at Novell.

My brothers, Dee and Robert, and my sisters, Patcee, Kittie, Dorothy, and Debbie. They saw the events described on these pages unfold in my life and have always been supportive of me and happy for my successes.

My mother-in-law, Rose Warne. She raised a wonderful daughter and always showed me love and appreciation. At the age of 97, she is still a shining example to all.

Steve and Barb Young. They have always been and always will be among my greatest and dearest friends.

To my eternal companion and best pal: God gave me a most treasured gift when I met you, Linda. I love your laugh, your smile, your intelligence, your goodness—indeed, you are the human embodiment of charity, the pure love of Christ. I will love you forever.

Dr. Linda Bradford has had a massive role in in helping me put this project together. She is a great writer and constantly provided outstanding feedback on style and substance. Linda even came up with this book title. We have laughed for years about how she is so gifted at creating book titles. Well, this one was a real game changer.

To my great friends and business colleagues: You have influenced my life, and your examples shine out clearly in this book: Jim Waldorf, Jim Walsh, Shannon Heward, Sharlene Anderson Scott Sandell, Shawn Lindquist, Steve Wozniak, Eric Schmidt, Ray Noorda, Scott McKinley, Mark Newman, David Flynn, Rick White, Karl Engemann, Larry King, Shawn King, Jim Patenaude,

Steve and Barb Young, Tom Smith, Mike and Jackie Leavitt, Ray Bingham, Malcolm Gladwell, Tom Judd, Paul Engemann, Stephen MR Covey, Scott Cutler, Ron Riddle, David Fretz, Mitt Romney, Larry Sonsini, Jon Huntsman, Jr, Jeff Hawn, Jim Dawson, Dennis Wolf, Hylton Van Zyl, George Boutros, Frank Quattrone, Erin Schurtz, David Checketts, Bill Gates, Greg Butterfield, Gary Hecker, Richard Rife, Vish Mishra, Donny and Debby Osmond, Dale Sutherland, Gary Kolman, Lane Martin, Lee Johnson, Jim Herrmann, Sterling Tanner, Governor Gary Herbert, Alan Rudd, Senator Orrin Hatch, Audrey Bailey, Jan Newman, and Richard King.

To the true spiritual giants in my life: You have always instilled in me a desire to be a better person. Thanks to Truman Madsen, Mel Hammond, Craig Zwick, Tom Bangert, and Monte McKeon.

To all of you in my network: You have been a blessing in my life. Thanks for connecting with me and making my life better.

—David Bradford